Country Roads ~ of ~ SOUTHERN CALIFORNIA

A Guide Book from Country Roads Press

Country Roads
~ of ~
# SOUTHERN CALIFORNIA

Arline Inge

Illustrated by
Cliff Winner

Country Roads Press
CASTINE • MAINE

Country Roads of Southern California

Published by Country Roads Press
P.O. Box 286, Lower Main Street
Castine, Maine 04421

Text and cover design by Edith Allard.
Cover illustration by Victoria Sheridan.
Illustrations by Cliff Winner.
Typesetting by Camden Type 'n Graphics.

ISBN 1-56626-076-0

Library of Congress Cataloging-in-Publication Data
Inge, Arline.
Country Roads of Southern California / Arline Inge ; illustrator, Cliff Winner.
p. cm.
Includes index.
ISBN 1-56626-076-0 : $9.95
1. California, Southern—Tours. 2. Automobile travel—California, Southern—Guidebooks. I. Title.
F867.I54 1995
917.94'9—dc20 94-45106
CIP

Printed in the United States of America.
10 9 8 7 6 5 4 3 2 1

To Virginia Miessner—traveler, writer, editor,
and the one with the bright ideas.

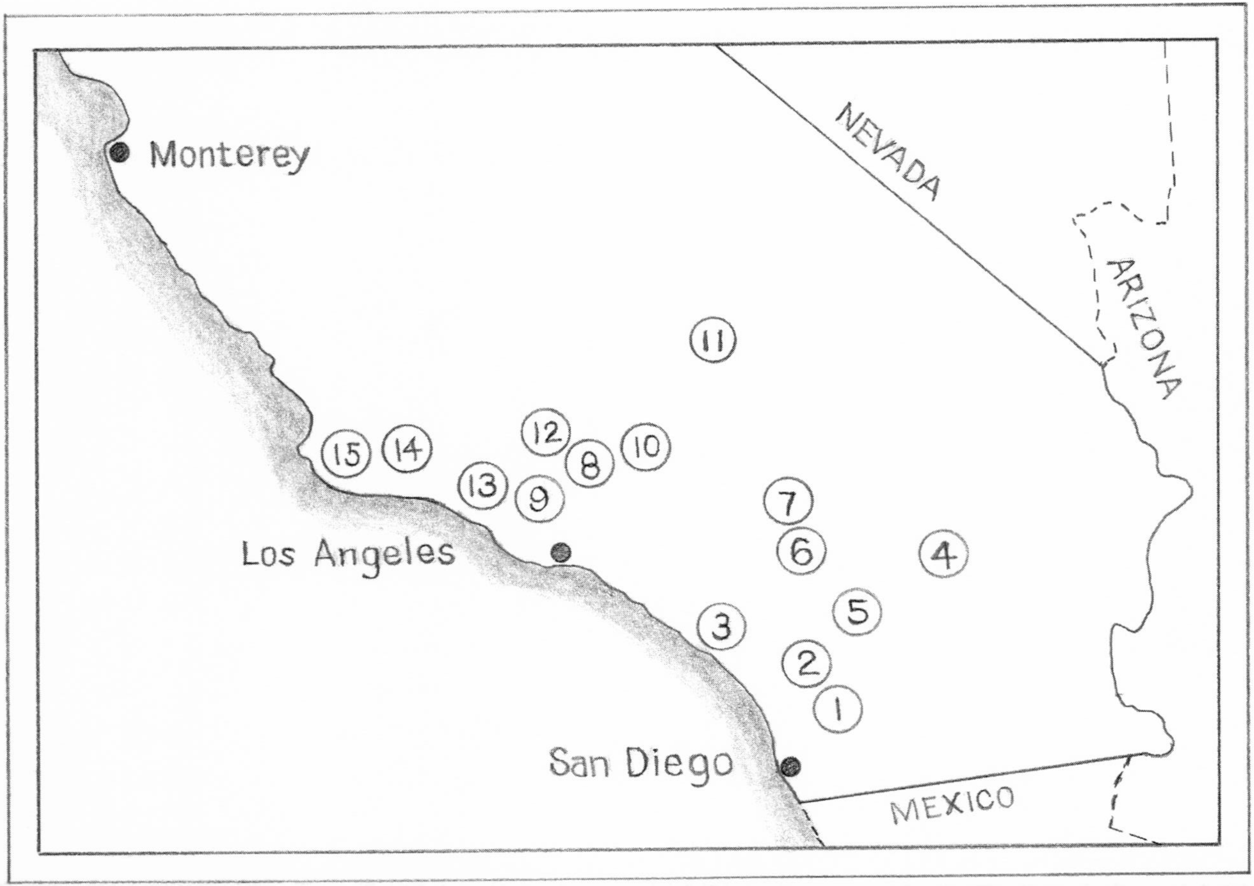
Monterey
NEVADA
ARIZONA
Los Angeles
San Diego
MEXICO
1
2
3
4
5
6
7
8
9
10
11
12
13
14
15

Contents

(& Key to Southern California Country Roads)

Introduction

Improvement makes great roads, but the crooked roads without improvement are roads of genius.

—William Blake

I've spent a lifetime in Southern California and never thought about country roads. I've thought in terms of Sunday drives and outdoor getaways. I've never said to my husband, "Let's go to the country." Instead I've said, "Let's go skiing this weekend." Or, "I feel like a drive in the desert." Or, "Let's go taste some wines." And so has everyone else—which could explain the raised eyebrows when I told my friends I planned to write about our country roads.

The exception was Virginia Miessner, a fellow writer and old friend from UCLA days. Virginia grew up in Kansas and knows a country road when she sees one. One night we sat down, spread out a map of Southern California, and looked at all the exciting places we'd visited during years of family outings and vacations. Between us, we'd covered dozens of beautiful country roads with fascinating things to do along the way.

Southern California country roads lead to ghost towns, gold mines, desert moonscapes, spectacular lakes, old missions, wildflower fields, wineries, ski slopes, hidden beaches, antique malls, real country villages, and engaging tourist towns. They squeeze down canyons, up stagecoach routes, and along earthquake faults. Some follow the footsteps of American Indians, padres, pioneers, prospectors, and early ranchers. They weave the routes and sights along the way into a living history of the rancho and mission days that shaped the southland.

Taking a yellow highlighter to the map, Virginia and I traced fifteen routes from San Diego to Santa Barbara Counties. We chose them for scenery and variety and because they lead to our favorite places. Then we drove every inch of road and wrote down every turn we made. May you never come to an unmarked fork and find that your map doesn't bother to show that unnamed road (we wish we'd had this guide). We also noted the addresses and phone numbers for great places to see and for chambers of commerce that will send out their visitor's guides on request. In country towns, they'll even chat about the place by phone.

We tried for 100 percent country roads, but that proved an impossible dream. In some places, we had to patch our routes together with short stretches of four-lane highway, even a few miles of freeway. We even developed a perverse affection for freeways as magic carpets to gentler roads ahead.

Our trips range from about 20 to 100 miles in length. You could easily drive the longest in three hours if you never got out of the car. But that's hardly the point. Some of the trips hold more temptations along the road than anyone can handle in a day. Even with an early start to build in dawdling time, you may need to save some stops for another trip or think about staying overnight for an extra day.

Bring a good map along to keep you on track in case you decide to wander off on detours along the way. Pack drinks and snacks. Restaurants tend to peter out in the country, but picnic spots are just around the corner. If you're bound for the mountains in winter, check with the Highway Patrol for snow warnings and always carry chains.

Not knowing where readers may be coming from, we've begun our mileage estimates from the start of each route, and we've included prominent freeway and highway departure points. Obviously, the mileage counts do not include your round-trip from home.

Thumb through our pages and plot your course. Southern California's country roads are filled with beauty and surprises, and they're out there waiting for you.

1 ~

Easy As Apple Pie

From Cuyamaca Rancho State Park to Julian

Getting Started: From San Diego, take the Descanso exit off I-8.

Route: From Descanso, take State 79 to Cuyamaca Rancho State Park and then to Julian. About twenty-five miles.

Highlights: *Enjoy the wilderness of Cuyamaca Rancho State Park. Sample the famous apple pies in Julian. Browse cunning collectibles and gift shops. Tour a gold mine. Revel in a Renoiresque spring landscape of apple blossoms and wildflowers. Come in fall to fill your shopping bags with apples, pears, and pumpkins from the farm stands.*

From the moment you leave busy I-8 at Descanso and turn onto countrified State 79, you'll be lazing past small horse and cattle ranches and mountain homes of folks who aren't bothered by the sight of an abandoned water heater on a neighbor's porch. You're heading up to Cuyamaca Rancho State Park's world of giant oaks, incense cedars, white firs and pines, willow-bordered streams, and open meadows. Only one paved road (you're on it) disturbs the wilderness. It runs for about seven miles straight through the park and continues on to Julian. Except for the campgrounds and ranger information centers, the rancho has been left to the mule deer, raccoons, coyotes, gray foxes, bobcats, and mountain lions.

In 1772, Don Pedro Fages, an early soldier-explorer and California governor, discovered these summer hunting grounds of the Kumeya'ay Indians while pursuing deserters from the San Diego Presidio. White settlers followed, first coexisting with the Indians but eventually driving them out onto nearby reservations. Had Fages and his men arrived a century later, instead of hunting down prisoners they would have been hunting for riches.

In 1870, the prospectors moved south from Julian, hammering their way through these untamed hills in search of gold-bearing quartz. The big strike came at Stonewall Mine here on Cuyamaca Rancho. Before it played out in 1892, the mine yielded up $2 million in bullion (in the days when gold went for about $18 an ounce) and employed 200 miners at a time.

When you reach the park entrance, go into the small museum in the rock-walled mansion of the Ralph Dyar family, the last owners of the ranch. The pinched faces of the Stonewall miners look down at you from the walls. Other exhibits track man's impact on these mountains from Indian times through mining days. For an overview of local ecology, stop at the Paso Picacho Interpretive Center a little farther up the road.

To see what remains of the Stonewall Mine, watch for the sign on the right side of the road and follow it four miles past the equestrian campground to the end. The forest has done a good job of reclaiming the sizable town that sprang up at the edge of the pit, but you can still see the 633-foot main shaft and a giant winch behind a high wire fence. The hammering of a woodpecker in the distance is a far cry from the clang and clatter of the mine that spawned a town of 500 in the early 1870s. On a bulletin board near the shaft, you'll get a good idea of the urban amenities—post office, hotel, and library—

that once stood on this empty carpet of pine needles under the trees.

If you've gotten an early start and the weather looks clear, you might fit in a bracing three-hour round-trip hike to the park's highest point, 6,500-foot Mount Cuyamaca, for a dazzling view of the Salton Sea, the Pacific Ocean, and Mexico. The trail starts at the Paso Picacho picnic grounds. A word of caution: When hiking here or in other California wilderness areas, be aware of the ever-present danger of encountering mountain lions or cougars. A hiker was fatally attacked by a cougar in the park in 1994. A safety pamphlet entitled "Living with Mountain Lions" is available from the California Department of Fish and Game. Some advice from the experts: Don't hike alone. Keep children close by. Do not approach a lion. Do not run from a lion. Do not crouch or bend over. Stand and face the animal and make eye contact.

When you're ready to complete the next ten miles to Julian, follow State 79 to the end of the park past the trout fishermen at Cuyamaca Lake and continue through the forested mountains to Julian. If you come into town for the autumn harvest, the road will be one farm stand after another heaped with fragrant apples, pears, pumpkins, and jugs of cider. On October weekends, there's a harvest festival in town.

At the height of its good fortune in the late 1800s, Julian rivaled San Diego in size and influence, and there was talk of making it the county seat. The first gleam of placer gold was found in a prospector's pan in 1869 at nearby Coleman Creek. A year later, the opening of the George Washington Mine brought 1,000 prospectors to comb the hills for their share of a southern mother lode that was to produce $15 million worth of bullion.

It was no time before Julian's muddy Main Street had wooden sidewalks running past saloons, stores, and bawdy houses to serve the tent city that sprang up in the hills. Finer

Harvesting apples for one of those famous Julian apple pies

buildings of brick and wood followed as the gold piled up. A few of those buildings, such as the tastefully restored Julian Hotel and the Julian Pioneer Museum, are still standing by the grace of two farsighted ranchers who refused to let Julian become a ghost town when the gold dwindled away in the 1880s.

Taking advantage of its 4,300-foot elevation and four-season climate, they brought in apple and pear trees, and for the next century Julian, supported by its thriving orchards, was a quiet agricultural center and a rural retreat for nearby San Diegans.

Then came the statewide U. S. Bicentennial celebration of 1976, and the old boomtown's historic past and appealing rural present kindled visitor interest and lit the flame under the town's bake ovens. Today Julian's quaint streets and restaurants and bakeries, which sell its famous pies, are so jammed, especially on weekends, that some of the 2,000 residents of the surrounding area (if they're not involved in the tourist trade) simply hole up in their houses along the wooded back roads and wait for the window-shoppers to go home. Four-block-long Main Street and a few side streets are lined with collectible and antique shops, some in adorable old cottages. The town also has an Indian shop, a working cider mill, a candy store, the usual T-shirt emporiums, and more. But the most fun is scouting out the bakeries and deciding where to have your juicy wedge of Julian apple pie. Choose between golden-brown crust or generous crumb, but be sure to have it à la mode.

The first apples planted here, McIntosh and Delicious, won prizes at the Chicago World's Fair of 1893. Since then growers have put in dozens of varieties, ensuring a succession of ripening fruit during the season. What then, you may ask, is a Julian apple? Answer: Any apple grown in Julian. But truth to tell, as one baker confides, the mystique of the Julian apple pie has outstripped the local apple supply, and pies you get after the season might be made with imported fruit.

Ask three people who bakes the best, and you'll get three impassioned opinions: "Apple Alley, definitely. Theirs is tarter and has a thin, crisp crust because they dust cornmeal on the bottom crust." Or, "Who's kidding who? Julian Pie Company's is the crispest." Or, "Check out Mom's. She taught every other baker in town."

Everyone does stop at Mom's Pies, Etc. on Main Street between Washington and B Streets to watch the bakers in their glassed-in kitchen. At the back of the busy dining room, a chatty helper, who must have been chosen for her kindly demeanor, discourses on the merits of the Julian pie while peeling, coring, and slicing apples by the bucket at a Rube Goldberg contraption. Mom's immutable recipe is posted on the front window for all to read: two and a half pounds of sliced fruit per pie and six ounces of dough each for top and bottom is the gist of it.

Julian has been declared a National Historic District. For a guided tour of the town and surrounding roads, hop a horse-drawn buggy at the corner of Main and Washington Streets. You'll want to drop in at the Julian Drug Store for an old-fashioned malted at the wide marble counter. (It stands on the site of an 1886 building, but the drugstore has been here only since the 1930s.)

Be sure to go into the fascinating Julian Pioneer Museum around the corner on Washington Street. Part of it is in a brick building dating from 1875 that was first the town brewery and later a blacksmith's shop. Be prepared to lose your sense of time among the odds and ends that form a picture of life in the 1800s—relics such as photos of the town fathers, antique mining equipment, household goods, and period clothing. The museum also has the biggest collection of vintage lace in California.

A little row of antique shops across the street from the museum complements the collection with bric-a-brac you can take home. Don't miss the rabbit warren of closet-size rooms crammed with curios at Applewood & Company. At the opposite end of town, on a small rise at the corner of Main and B Streets, stands the beautifully restored two-story, white-clapboarded Julian Hotel, established in 1869. In the glory days when the famous Overland Butterfield Stagecoach stopped across the street, the hotel lodged dignitaries such as Ulysses S. Grant. Unfortunately, when we were there, the front door was locked against casual visitors so that only guests could enjoy its plant-filled Victorian lobby and lovingly restored bedrooms.

The remains of the hard-rock gold mines still honeycomb the mountainsides, but very few are working. You can get a good mining demonstration at the Eagle and High Peak Gold Mine of 1897. Drive back along Main Street to C Street, turn left, and continue for six blocks to the old work site. The hour-and-a-half tour takes you through 1,000 feet of tunnels that led to ore worth $3.5 million over the years. It shows how ore is extracted from the quartz rock, refined, and molded into bars. You can even try your hand at panning, which, after all, was how the first gold was discovered here.

To leave Julian, follow State 78/79 (two routes merge here for a stretch) down the hill past orchards and farm stands. Where State 78 leaves State 79, turn right for a two-mile detour to a small Indian mission at Santa Ysabel. This graceful snow-white church is contemporary, but it stands on the site of an 1818 *asistencia,* or branch, of the mother mission in San Diego, which was established to minister to the Indians on the surrounding reservations. At one side, you'll see a sculpture memorializing the two bronze bells that hung from a crude wooden stand outside the church when it was a primitive straw-roofed chapel. The bells mysteriously disappeared, and only the corroded pieces of the clappers were found. You can see them in the low case on your right as you enter the chapel museum.

On leaving the mission, backtrack to the junction and turn right (west) on State 78 past another local landmark, Dudley's Bakery. Customers come from as far away as San Diego to stock up on Dudley's seventeen varieties of fresh-baked bread. State 78 will take you to State 67 and back to I-8 and San Diego.

In the Area

Cuyamaca Rancho State Park, 12551 Highway 79, Descanso, CA 92106. 619-765-0755.

California Department of Fish and Game, 1416 Ninth Street, Sacramento, CA 95814. 916-653-7203.

Julian Chamber of Commerce (information and accommodations), Main and Washington Streets, PO Box 413, Julian, CA 92036. 619-765-1857.

Julian Pioneer Museum, Washington at Fourth, Julian, CA 92036. 619-765-0227.

Eagle and High Peak Gold Mine, Top of C Street, Julian, CA 92036. 619-765-0227.

Julian Hotel, 2032 Main Street, Julian, CA 92036. 619-765-0201 or 800-724-5854.

Mom's Pies, Etc., 1229 Main Street, Julian, CA 92036. 619-765-2472.

Apple Alley, 2122 Main Street, Julian, CA 92036. 619-765-2532.

Julian Pie Company, 2225 Main Street, Julian, CA 92036. 619-765-2449.

Applewood & Company, 2804 Washington, Julian, CA 92036. 619-765-1185.

Mission Santa Ysabel, State 79, Santa Ysabel, CA 92070. 619-765-0810.

Dudley's Bakery, 30218 Highway 78/79, Santa Ysabel, CA 92070. 619-765-0488 or 800-225-3348.

2 ~

A Road Full of Marvels

From Mission San Luis Rey to Palomar Mountain and Temecula

Getting Started: At Oceanside, take the Mission Avenue exit off I-5.

Route: From Mission San Luis Rey, take State 78 to the San Diego Wild Animal Park and San Pasqual Battlefield. Take State 78, 79, and State 76 to Palomar Mountain and Mission San Antonio de Pala. From Pala, take County 516 to Temecula. About 100 miles.

Highlights: *Tour the king of missions, San Luis Rey, then head for the San Diego backcountry. Visit the San Diego Wild Animal Park and historic San Pasqual Battlefield. Climb up through Cleveland National Forest to silver-domed Palomar Observatory and back down through Pauma Valley orange groves to the comely San Antonio de Pala Indian mission. Prowl 350 antique shops in Temecula and finish with a valley wine country tour.*

From the Mission Avenue exit off I-5, turn east to start the day at magnificent Mission San Luis Rey, the largest of all the California missions. In about four miles, you'll see the mission's majestic white colonnade and brilliant blue cupola looming on a grassy rise where it was once surrounded by fifteen square miles of ranch land. The entrance drive, Peyri Road, is named for the padre who headed the mission for thirty-four years.

Even though it is second in the mission lineup after San Diego de Alcalá, San Luis Rey de Francia (honoring Saint

Louis IX of France) was actually one of the last missions in California's twenty-one-mission chain. It was founded in 1798, almost thirty years after the San Diego mission, to reach the Indians between San Diego and Mission San Juan Capistrano. At its peak, the lives of 2,000 Indians revolved around its church and workshops, which covered six acres. Starting with a few pickaxes, some primitive plowshares, and a few animals borrowed from other missions, San Luis Rey raised more livestock than any other mission and was second in the production of grain.

If the mission developed rapidly, its downfall came almost as fast. After the secularization of the missions in the 1830s, cattle were slaughtered for their hides and the land was partitioned among the Indians—only to be stolen from them. The neglected buildings were eventually sold for $2,437.

What was left of the buildings was returned to the Catholic Church in 1865 by presidential decree. The mission was restored on the old foundations in 1893, down to the thick adobe walls and heavy beamed ceilings. The sparkling buildings you see today are from that reconstruction. When you go into the church, notice the intricately worked wooden dome over the transept. It is the only one like it remaining in the mission chain.

Next door to the church is a richly stocked museum showing the life of both the neophytes, as mission Indians were called, and the clergy. You'll see how the Indians made candles and soap, how hides were tanned, what tools were used to till the soil, and how kitchens functioned in those days. One of the museum's great treasures is a collection of eighteenth- and nineteenth-century embroidered vestments from Spain.

From the museum, walk to your right along the wall and look through the archway of the private retreat garden. You'll see the first pepper tree in California, brought by a Peruvian sea captain in 1830. To the right toward the street are ornate steps leading to the excavated Indian laundry, where water flowed out of the mouths of gargoyles from nearby streams.

On leaving, turn right onto Mission Avenue and left onto El Camino Real to State 78 east. Continue on to Via Rancho Parkway and keep heading east to San Pasqual Road and San Pasqual Valley Road (you'll be on State 78 again), following the signs to the San Diego Wild Animal Park. Nurseries growing palms and Christmas trees appear on the same stretch of road. A sign advertising beef jerky pops up just before you see Chico's brimming farm stand in a big traffic island formed by two roads. The corn "so tender that you can eat it raw from the cob" truly is, and the apricots from the local orchards are like honey. If you pass up Chico's, you'll have another chance at the farm stand on the edge of a lettuce field in front of the animal park.

You could spend your whole day at the 2,000-acre San Diego Wild Animal Park, which includes dozens of wildlife and botanical displays, aviaries, and animal shows. Provided you don't mind shelling out a full day's admission for a short visit, you can survey the main attractions aboard the Wgasa Bush Line Monorail. This fifty-minute, five-mile guided tour circles the re-created plains and swamps of Africa and Asia, where animals such as elephants, giraffes, gazelles, oryx, wildebeests, and rhinos are allowed to run free.

San Pasqual Valley Road (State 78) continues on through rolling hills to the often-overlooked but fascinating San Pasqual Battlefield State Historic Park. The museum is open Friday through Sunday, but even if it's closed, you can walk up to the wall near the entrance and look out over the cornfields to the low hills in back. The American Dragoons led by Brigadier General Stephen Kearny rode over that ridge to face Mexico's Californiano forces led by Major Andrés Pico one cold, rainy December dawn in 1846. It proved to be one of the bloodiest battles of the Mexican War. The battle was a painful

Residents of the San Diego Wild Animal Park, where the animals roam free and the visitors stay behind bars

defeat for the Americans and a victory that came too late for Mexico. In the museum, a pair of stained-glass windows tell the story. One shows an American with firearms, and the other shows a Californiano armed with a lance. In a surprise turnaround, the American muskets and cannons misfired (the powder was damp), and the Californianos polished them off with lances made from knives tied to willow poles. But Pico's victory was hollow. He soon learned that Los Angeles had already surrendered to the Americans and Mexico had all but lost California.

From the museum, State 78 leads past pleasant orchards and up the San Pasqual grade to the horse country of Ramona. If you like Mexican food and barbecue, look no further than Ramona's lineup of restaurants after the road turns to go through town. From Ramona, you'll take a thirteen-mile meander toward the Santa Rosa Mountains past pastures, poultry farms, and ranches advertising llamas and pygmy goats for sale. When you get to the local landmark, Dudley's Bakery, at the junction of State 79, you'll be only seven miles east of Julian, the apple pie town, which we visited in Chapter 1.

Everyone stops at Dudley's to inhale the heavenly aromas of baking bread (seventeen varieties daily) and to watch a small army of bakers at work. After coffee and Danish, take State 79 north to the small white Mission Santa Ysabel on your right. Bells on poles like shepherds' crooks, like the one at this mission gate, used to mark El Camino Real (the royal road), which went from mission to mission up the California coast. Santa Ysabel was established in 1818 as an *asistencia,* or country outpost of the San Diego mission. The immaculate church, with exuberant Indian murals inside, is a twentieth-century replacement. Out front is a monument to the famous lost bells of Santa Ynez, which hung from a crude wooden stand outside the simple rush-roofed adobe structure that was the early church. The oldest bells in California, they had been bought from a mission in Baja California for six burro loads of hay and barley. They disappeared one day in 1926, and only the clappers have been found. As you enter the one-room mission museum, you'll see corroded remains of the clappers in the glass case by the door to your right.

From the mission, it is a scenic twenty-one miles to Palomar Observatory high in the Cleveland National Forest. At the fork in the road, veer to the left onto State 76 to skirt the southwest bank of Lake Henshaw, a desert lake with treeless shores that only a fisherman could love. And judging by the flock of boats on the lake angling for bass, bluegills, and catfish, the fishermen must love this spot. For permission to put your boat in the water, drop in at the Lake Henshaw Resort store across the street.

In about nine miles, start watching for the sharp right turn onto County S6 and start your zigzag up through the dense black-pine forests to the mile-high observatory. From the road, the dome looks like a toy, but it grows inch by inch as you get closer. Still, you haven't seen anything until you've walked up the path from the parking lot and looked up at the twelve-story-high silver ball towering against the clear mountain sky. The great dome of the Pantheon in Rome is only ten feet taller. Don't expect a panoramic view from here (you get that on the road going down); the observatory grounds lie in a small mountain meadow away from the edge of the hill. Palomar Observatory, an arm of Caltech in Pasadena, was opened in 1948 to house the 200-inch Hale telescope, the most powerful telescope in the world. Since then, the 530-ton giant has been improved with sensitive new position sensors and computers. By day, the great dome is kept closed to protect the Hale from heat and rain. At night, the dome's twin shutters, each weighing 125 tons, roll open to allow the telescope to continue its search of the universe. A special lubricating system keeps the bearings so free of friction that the Hale can be moved to follow the stars by a mere one-twelfth-horsepower motor or by the steady pressure of one finger. The base of the building, off-limits to visitors, holds computers, photographic plate storage, generators,and other support systems.

You can inspect the giant at rest during the day from a glassed-in visitors gallery in the observatory. Then look into the adjacent museum and learn how the Hale has enlarged astronomers' view of the universe through amazing feats of photography. The giant circular cement slab on the museum floor is the exact size of the telescope's 200-inch light-gathering mirror.

To continue toward Temecula, go back down County S6 and turn right (west) on State 76. It leads to the broad Pauma Valley, whose patchwork of orange groves runs up to the tops of the hills. The decorative twelve-foot-high pink, red, and white oleander bushes along the road are windbreaks. The oleanders down the middle of the road protect against the lights of oncoming traffic. As the groves thin out, watch for a small road that should say Pala Mission Drive (you never know around here). It slants off to the right and takes you to the Pala Indian Reservation and everyone's dream of a country mission, San Antonio de Pala.

In 1827, Padre Peyri of Mission San Luis Rey described the mission at Pala this way: "At a distance of seven leagues toward the northeast, at the entry of the Sierra Madre, the Mission [of San Luis Rey] has a station called San Antonio de Pala, with a church, dwellings, and granaries and a few fields where wheat, corn, beans, garbanzos, and other leguminous plants are grown. There is also a vineyard and an orchard of various fruits and olives, for which there is sufficient irrigation, the water being from the stream which runs to the vicinity of this mission."

This well-tended *asistencia* is the last one in California still serving the Indian congregation for which it was built. When construction was begun in 1810, Indians climbed the slopes of Palomar Mountain to cut cedars for the roof beams, hauling trees down the mountain with oxen and horses or carrying them on their own shoulders. One hundred fifty years later after a turbulent history of damage by earthquakes, flooding, and neglect, a new generation of Indian builders went back up the mountain to haul down cedar trees for the last restoration in 1954. The freestanding bell tower, with its two original bells hung one above the other, was modeled on one in Juarez, Mexico, and is a favorite subject for photographers and artists. The long, narrow brick-floored chapel with rough-hewn cedar rafters and murals adorning lumpy adobe walls is very much as it was in the beginning. The murals, with an acorn theme prevalent in Indian art, were pretty well obliterated when an overzealous padre neatened up the interior in 1903 by having them whitewashed. An Indian artist successfully re-created these flowing designs from old photos.

The museum and gift shop are worth a visit. You'll see relics from the original church and handicrafts currently being made for sale by reservation residents. While we were there, the shopkeeper was sewing a pair of miniature leather moccasins for a souvenir key chain.

To head for Temecula, turn right out of the mission, continue one block, and turn right again at Pala Temecula Road (County S16). You'll pass the tribal headquarters and the town will soon disappear as the road runs through hilly ranch land for nine miles to the outskirts of Temecula. Just before you get to the intersection of State 79, you'll see Rainbow Canyon Road. A left turn here leads to the luxuriant grounds of the Temecula Creek Inn, a relaxing place to spend the night before tackling Temecula. To get into town, turn left at the intersection of State 79 and prepare for a culture shock.

This is Front Street in "old town" Temecula. In six short blocks, between Moreno Road and Second Street, the Old West comes alive in 350 antique, collectible, and gift shops. Although a few of the buildings come honestly by their weathered frontier-style exteriors, the antique phenomenon here is new. Up until 1985, there were only about six antique stores in the whole town.

Temecula has only recently become a tourist attraction. From 1904 to 1964, it was a a rip-roaring cowboy town and grain-and-cattle-shipping center for the 87,500-acre ranch owned by cattle baron Walter Vail. The new housing tracts, medical and electronics companies, and vineyards and citrus groves came after the sale of the Vail Ranch in 1964.

The Temecula Museum, on Main Street just east of Front Street, contains a model of the town as it looked in 1914. You'll recognize some of the houses as you walk around town. At the corner of Front and Main stood the First National Bank, which is still in the same spot, only now it's painted grass green and houses a popular restaurant called the Bank of Mexican Food. After seeing the miniature Victorian gingerbread Welty/Temecula Hotel from 1882, you'll recognize the real thing on the north side of Main Street down toward Murrieta Creek. It's now a private home.

A walking tour brochure, available at the museum and other places around town, will help you sort out old and new Temecula and is a useful guide to the bewildering but tantalizing world of antique shopping. The shops also are listed in the Temecula Visitor's Guide, which has details of Temecula's May Hot Big Air Balloon and Wine Festival, among other events, and is available from the Chamber of Commerce. Most shoppers go up one side of Front Street and down the other, but if you're in a hurry, just look in at Temecula Mercantile, whose twenty-six stalls occupy an 1891 brick building with the original granite hitching post intact, or the Chaparral Antique Mall, with a wagon wheel outside, at Sixth and Front. The latter has furniture, bric-a-brac, clothing, dolls, china, and jewelry for sale by seventy different dealers. Granny's Attic Antique Mall, the biggest antique store in town, is in an enormous industrial shed with more than 125 stalls and loads of old furniture just across Murrieta Creek. Although you can walk to it, you'll need your car to carry your purchases, so drive north on Front Street, then turn left over the creek on Rancho California Road, left on Vincent Moraga, and left on Felix Valdez.

Local historians think that the name Temecula means "place where the sun shines through the mist." That morning mist and the moist Pacific Ocean breeze wafting through the Rainbow Gap to the southwest now provides ideal conditions for the almost 3,000 acres of sunbaked vines of the new Temecula wine country.

A tour of the wineries and a picnic on the grounds is a favorite pastime for San Diegans, who consider Temecula their own domain, even though it is over the line in Riverside County. From Front Street, turn right (east) on Rancho California Road past shiny new suburbs. The vines will suddenly appear, and you'll see driveways running up from Rancho California to the wineries on the hills.

Most of the wineries offer tastings for a small fee, which includes a wineglass to take home; some have deli picnic items to go with your wine. The giant Calloway Winery gives a bang-up professional tour of the winemaking process. Smaller outfits may have a more personal approach, and some offer only tastings with a look at the fermenting tanks and aging barrels. Pick up a free wine country map and guide at a restaurant, shop, or winery, or you may request one in advance from the Temecula Valley Vintners Association. Some of the smaller wineries are closed to the public on weekdays, so check the guide before planning a visit. Wine country is only four miles from town, so it makes sense to go back and forth between antiquing and wine tasting. For our purposes, we'll start with the wineries on the right side of the road and hit the ones on the left on the way back.

As serendipity would have it, the most alluring winery on the route is at the top of the first driveway on the right. The Mediterranean villa of the Thornton Winery is usually crowded, and on Sunday afternoons a jazz concert is held on its big central patio. This is the only winery with a restaurant. Café Champagne serves trendy California cooking for lunch and dinner on the terrace overlooking the vines or inside in a bistro setting. Thornton used to be the Culbertson Winery, and it still sells Culbertson's highly respected Champagnes along with its own varied list.

Next on the road is the driveway to the Baily tasting room, which you can skip if you plan to visit Baily's working winery farther down the road. The next drive leads to the

Cilurzo Winery, a Temecula old-timer whose vines date from the late 1960s. A Cilurzo family member is usually on hand to talk about the latest bottlings in the cluttered tasting room. Try the reds, especially the cabernet sauvignon and the merlot. Cilurzo's neighbor, the Santa Margarita winery, is a small newcomer making its name with cabernet sauvignon. Turn right on Madera del Playa to reach this winery.

Back on the main road, the appealing white gingerbread farmhouse of Maurice Carrie of Winery has inviting green lawns and a picnic gazebo. Inside, at the fanciest gift shop–tasting room in the valley, you can sample a wide selection of wines including chardonnay, cabernet sauvignon, and Muscat Canelli. Tours are not offered on a regular basis.

From here, Rancho California Road takes you for a ride through vineyards that stand side by side with flourishing orange groves. Turn right onto Glenoaks Road and watch for the tiny Filsinger Winery on your right. This winery specializes in Champagnes and still white wines.

At De Portola Road, turn right and take the driveway up to the Keyways in the long, low mission-style winery on your left. You'll enjoy Gamay Beaujolais, Muscat Canelli, and cabernet sauvignon poured at a tasting bar that came out of an old Temecula saloon. The winery dates back only to the late eighties, but its vineyards are the oldest in the valley. Horticulturists had a hunch that the climate was right and were experimenting here forty years ago.

If your car can take a pretty rough dirt road, continue a short way down De Portola Road to dusty Pauba Road. The tree-shaded Baily Winery is at the top of the hill. This small family enterprise specializes in whites and is proud of its Montage, a blend of sauvignon blanc and Semillon. The winery also operates the Baily Wine Country Café in town, serving gourmet California cuisine with a list of Temecula wines that includes the best ones from its competitors.

Retrace your steps to the initial cluster of wineries on Rancho California Road and turn right on Calle Contento for a magnificent view of valley and mountains at the contemporary quarters of the Temecula Crest Winery. The winery opened in 1994 with cabernet sauvignon and whites including chardonnay and white zinfandel. An equally stunning view awaits you at Clos du Muriel. Its informal tasting counter in the midst of tanks and shipping cartons offers an unusually generous ten tastes per person.

You'll think you're in Italy when you see the red-tiled roof of the Mount Palomar Winery. Inside, the tasting room is cozy, its walls covered with ribbons won by its prize wines. The little back-room deli makes sandwiches to order, which you can enjoy in one of several intimate picnic areas. Mount Palomar concentrates on whites, but it produces others, including cabernet sauvignon, cream sherry, and port.

The next-to-the-last stop is Calloway, up a driveway bordered by roses. You can picnic here under a grape arbor looking down on vines in all directions. Unlike its neighbors, Calloway, with 800 acres of vineyards, is nationally known and has enough production to ship out of state in quantity. It is known for its whites, especially chardonnay. The last driveway on the road belongs to the modest Hart Winery, located in a redwood barn surrounded by storage barrels. Oenophiles come here especially for the unusual French varietals.

When it's time to start home, pick up I-15 off Rancho California Road at the edge of Temecula for points north and south.

In the Area

Mission San Luis Rey, 4050 Mission Avenue, San Luis Rey, CA 91068. 619-757-3651.

San Diego Wild Animal Park, 15600 San Pasqual Valley Road, Escondido, CA 92027. 619-231-0251.

San Pasqual State Historic Park, 15808 San Pasqual Valley Road, Escondido, CA 92027. 619-489-0076.

Dudley's Bakery, State 78/79, Santa Ysabel, CA 92070. 800-225-3348.

Mission Santa Ysabel, State 79, Santa Ysabel, CA 92070. 619-765-0810.

Palomar Observatory, County 6, Palomar Mountain, CA 92060. 619-742-2119.

Mission San Antonio de Pala, Pala Mission Road, Pala, CA 92059. 619-742-3317.

Temecula Valley Chamber of Commerce, 27450 Ynez Road, Suite 104, Temecula, CA 92591. 909-676-5090.

Temecula Valley Vintners Association (wine country guide) Box 1606, Temecula, CA 92593. 909-699-3626.

Temecula Museum, 41950 Main Street, Temecula, CA 92590. 909-676-0021.

Temecula Mercantile, 42049 Main Street, Temecula, CA 92590. 909-676-2722.

Chaparral Antique Mall, 28465 Front Street, Temecula, CA 92590. 909-676-0070.

Granny's Attic Antique Mall, 28450 Felix Valdez Avenue, Temecula, CA 92590. 909-699-9449.

Bank of Mexican Food, 28645 Front Street, Temecula, CA 92590. 909-676-6160.

Café Champagne, Thornton Winery, 32575 Rancho California Road, Temecula, CA 92590. 909-699-0099.

Baily Wine Country Cafe, 27644 Ynez Road, Temecula, CA 92591. 909-676-9567.

Temecula Creek Inn, 44501 Rainbow Canyon Road, Temecula, CA 92592. 909-694-1000.

Doubletree Suites Hotel, 29345 Rancho California Road, Temecula, CA 92591. 909-676-5656.

3 ~

Little Bit of Heaven

From San Juan Capistrano to Lake Elsinore and Perris

Getting Started: Take I-5 to the Father Junípero Serra exit in San Juan Capistrano.

Route: Follow the Ortega Highway (State 74) from San Juan Capistrano to Lake Elsinore and Perris. About fifty miles.

Highlights: *Begin at Mission San Juan Capistrano, where padres and Indians earned their place in heaven. Take a mountain drive to the hang-gliding capital of Lake Elsinore and the skydiving capital of Perris. Ride an old trolley at the Orange Empire Railway Museum.*

The centerpiece of San Juan Capistrano is the acknowledged jewel of California missions, founded in 1776 by Father Junípero Serra. As you approach the mission from Camino Capistrano, you'll come upon the great crumbling shell and the only dome remaining from the seven-domed stone church that stood here with all the grandeur of a cathedral. Indians built it stone by stone under the direction of a master mason from Mexico. Six years after it was finished, the earthquake of 1812 tore the church apart, killing forty worshipers at Mass. It was never rebuilt.

The crannies of the crumbling ruin became the home of the famous cliff swallows, which every year fly 6,000 miles from Goya, Argentina, to arrive on St. Joseph's Day, March 19. They repair their old nests with mud from irrigation ditches and ponds and leave for home on October 23. Of course, they don't always make it on the dot, but scientists still haven't figured how they do it at all. Fewer and fewer swallows have been coming back in recent years, daunted by the increasingly urban surroundings of the mission. But the faithful few are eagerly awaited on St. Joseph's Day, to be greeted with a colorful fiesta and a rendition of the old song "When the Swallows Come Back to Capistrano," which made the mission world famous in the forties.

Inside the mission gate is an active religious community. You can visit the oldest standing chapel in California, the only remaining church where Father Serra said Mass. Still in use for religious services, it is richly decorated with Indian murals and many treasures that were saved from the stone church. Father Serra's church, as well as the padres' living quarters and workshops, have been faithfully restored to give a picture of life as it was during the days when the mission was a bastion of civilization in the wilderness.

After the Catholic Church was forced to give up its property during the secularization of mission lands in the 1830s, many of the buildings fell into such disrepair that in 1845, a prominent rancher, William Forster, was able to buy the mission at auction for $710. It was the Forster family home until President Abraham Lincoln returned the mission to the Catholic Church in 1865.

You can get an idea of what the original stone church looked like before its demise if you walk back up Camino Capistrano to the imposing white parish church on the corner. Domes and all, it was built along the old lines in 1985. Bold floral murals painted by Indians in rose, aqua, and yellow brighten the stark interior.

If you're interested in architecture, go around the corner to Acjachema Street to see the mauve-and-beige public library designed by the eminent postmodernist architect Michael Graves to blend into the mission neighborhood. If you peek inside, you'll see the plush furnishings he designed as well, down to the lamps and secluded reading nooks with garden views.

Every town has "the other side of the tracks." Capistrano's is one of its most beloved neighborhoods. Continue down Camino Capistrano onto Del Obispo Street and turn right just after the Santa Fe tracks on Los Rios Street. You'll find plenty of parking on Los Rios. The more than a dozen eighteenth- and nineteenth-century houses of the Los Rios Historic District start here along a narrow street with overgrown gardens of hollyhocks, daisies, and old roses. Most of the little houses are occupied, some by descendants of the original owners.

Outside the Rios Adobe at 37181 Los Rios hangs a shingle that reads "Stephen M. Rios, Attorney-at-Law," making his the oldest residence in California continuously occupied by the same family. It was built for Feliciano Rios, a Spanish soldier stationed at the mission. At the railroad crossing, you will find a plaque diagramming the street and the most interesting places to visit. One of the most curious is an ancient board-and-batten bungalow with twenty-five old-time gasoline pumps lined up in the yard.

Back across the street is the O'Neill House, authentically furnished in a Victorian style. It's open for visits daily except Saturday and Monday. The house is headquarters for the local historical society, which conducts a tour of the Los Rios Historic District every Sunday at 1:00 P.M., leaving from Pedro's Tacos across the street from the mission.

By now you've probably noticed the old Capistrano depot by the tracks. Rubble from the mission after the 1812 earthquake supplied some of the building materials. Completed in 1895, the depot still sells train tickets and also houses the lively Rio Grande Bar & Grill, which serves drinks in an old dining car and meals on a broad deck overlooking the back fences of Los Rios Street. The other popular place to eat is the El Adobe Restaurant, at 31891 Camino Capistrano. President Richard Nixon was a regular there when he was at the San Clemente White House. The old house was once a stagecoach stop, but now the food is Mexican.

Then it's on to Lake Elsinore via the Ortega Highway (State 74), which you can catch at the entrance to the mission. It was named for José Ortega, a scout in the party of eighteenth-century explorer Gaspar de Portolá, who passed this way with Father Serra. Ortega discoverered the Golden Gate at San Francisco Bay.

This narrow two-lane road, built in the thirties, can be dangerous when drivers who know all the curves by heart come barreling along, so pull over wherever you can for tailgaters. As suburbia fades, you'll be in golden ranch country on the 40,000-acre Rancho Mission Viejo. Grazing cattle, citrus groves, plant nurseries, and vegetable fields occupy the broad valleys along the road for seven miles.

The terrain grows more unruly as you come to the entrance to Ronald W. Caspers Wilderness Park in the foothills of the Santa Ana Mountains. The park is not for kids or sissies. No one under eighteen is allowed, and mountain lion and rattlesnake warnings are posted at the gate. The park has regular campgrounds and equestrian camping under the oaks and sycamores. Hikes lead up to rugged canyons in the shadow of Saddleback Mountain.

Farther down the road, an unexpected traffic light slows cars for the turn into the Nichols Institute biotech center. Look up to the right, and you'll see a graceful mirrored building in the middle of the forest. Civilization ends here, as the Ortega Highway makes its way up to the pines of Cleveland National Forest.

Regulars on this road like to break up the drive with a picnic along the hidden creek at the leafy Lower San Juan Picnic Area. Watch for the sign to the steep, short road down on the left. After leaving the picnic grounds, keep your eyes on the curves for the next eleven miles. You may wonder about the blackened bushes sticking up from the greenery. This is forest fire country. Most trees eventually green up and grow over the bald spots, but the manzanitas never regain their deep mahogany color.

You'll pass several campgrounds just before reaching the summit of the road at 2,666 feet. Then suddenly you'll emerge from the forest to see the high desert terrain of the Elsinore Valley below. You've reached the famous hang-glider heaven in the Ortega Hills. Stop at the turnout at the edge of the hill, or park in the wide gravel lot of the Lookout Roadhouse Restaurant just ahead. On weekends it's packed with families watching the hang gliders ride the thermal updrafts in the open sky above pale blue Lake Elsinore. They rise as high as 14,000 feet.

The moment you open the car door, you'll feel the thermal lift. Behind you is a dirt road that winds up to the take-off point near Elsinore Peak. By scanning the skyline, you may be able to make out a tiny moving dot, which is the wind sock near the point where the hang gliders spring off the pine-covered cliffs to land where palm trees grow. Cross-country gliders have soared 50 miles to land at Hemet or Palm Springs, and a recent record was set at 160 miles to Needles. For a ringside seat at these spectacular aerial ballets, have a beer or a slice of Roadhouse Chocolate Suicide Cake on the deck or at the big picture window inside the restaurant.

From here the road drops swiftly to the lake past the hang-gliding landing field. Lake Elsinore is up to its optimum water level and wholeheartedly enjoyed by boaters, fishermen, and water-skiers. A $60 million lake management program has put an end to the lake's yo-yo performance of the past. The huge rectangle of water almost drained away in the 1950s, only to be flooded to overflowing by runoff from the mountains in 1980.

At the Ortega Junction at the bottom of the hill, turn left on Riverside Drive (still State 74) and continue past the entrance to the Lake Elsinore State Park Marina and Recreation Area to Lakeshore Drive. After Lakeshore Drive becomes Graham Avenue, look left for Elsinore's biggest earthbound tourist attraction, the weathered two-story Crescent Bath House, in peeling, faded Russian blue with mouldering lacy white Victorian trim. It dominates the corner at 201 West Graham as it has since 1887, when it was the finest spa in town. Elsinore was founded as a health resort at the site of hot sulfur mineral springs, where the Paiahche Indians used to soak their weary bones. The Indians called it "springs by the sea," a name disdained by pretentious developers who renamed it after the Danish castle in Shakespeare's *Hamlet*.

When the Crescent Bath House opened at the hot springs with 132° F Roman baths and mud rooms, it attracted celebrity soakers such as President Grover Cleveland, heavyweight champ John L. Sullivan, "Buffalo Bill" Cody, and actress Lillian Russell. The tubs are still up on the second floor, and the building is a National Historic Monument. Downstairs is a tempting antique shop called The Chimes, open only on Saturday and Sunday.

Kitty-corner across the street is the old Santa Fe Railroad Station where Crescent patrons would arrive in town. The last train came through in 1951, but there are still a few yards of track beside the station, as well as the ticket window inside. The ladies' waiting room is now the director's office. There was no special room for men, who waited outside by the tracks.

You can catch some skydiving, usually on weekends, at the Lake Elsinore Airport at the far end of the lake. We tend to skip this one because the next stop is Perris, with nonstop traffic in the skies.

Retrace your route to State 74 and turn right (north). The fifteen miles to Perris, past empty hills and auto repair shops, is so dismal that you would turn back if you didn't know what was waiting. But there's little traffic, and you'll soon be rolling in on Fourth Street, bound for the train museum and airport.

Start at the big Orange Empire Railway Museum near the airfield because you can see the divers dropping out of the sky while you climb in and out of the railway cars. Follow Fourth Street to A Street, then turn right to the biggest railroad museum in the western United States. If you come on a weekend when volunteers play railroad conductor and engineer, you'll be welcomed aboard the hissing, whistle-tooting trains for a run along two and a half miles of tracks laid out in the countryside. More than 200 locomotives, passenger coaches, boxcars, nostalgic trolleys, and adorable toy trains and scale models have been amassed here since the museum's modest beginnings in 1956.

You can walk through the old car barns and talk with the passionate train restorers while they tinker with the monster locomotives. Around the grounds you'll see horse-drawn cars from the 1870s, a Japanese trolley, old freight trains, a "modern" 1939 diesel locomotive, and trains you never knew existed. If you've ever wondered where the big Red Cars of the Pacific Electric Railway went to die, you'll be happy to find these old-timers spruced up here. The museum is actually located in the 1880s town of Pinacate, which once supplied the needs of the miners in the area. Two of the original buildings are left, and other old Perris-area houses have been moved in to make a small outdoor museum. In 1886, the Pinacate stop was moved to Perris a mile and a half away. The museum holds a colorful festival in April, when the train makes round-trips from Pinacate to the Perris station.

From the trains, it's no distance at all to the skydiving jump target. Go left on Mapes Road, then left on Goetz Road

Skydiving over Lake Elsinore

to the first terminal of the Perris Valley Airport. Drive in on the dirt road past the mosquito-like open-air ultralight planes.

Park near the edge of the runway near the hangar of the Perris Valley Sky Diving School. As many as 150 jumpers come here every week. You can watch the parade of planes taking off to empty their cargoes of jumpers into the blue at 12,500 feet. On a busy day, the Sky Van will be flying. Twenty-four jumpers, one after the other, walk out of the open back of the plane. The free fall looks endless, but it's actually only fifty seconds before the colorful canopies unfurl for the five-minute float to the field, where everyone seems to land gracefully feetfirst. At the far end of the airport, you'll see less intrepid jumpers taking off in tandem with an instructor from the hot-air balloons of Air Express. For a hot-air balloon ride over the countryside, you have to be here at sunrise.

Eight miles north of the city is its other big attraction, the Lake Perris State Recreation Area, with extensive campgrounds. From the airport, continue on Goetz Road, turn left on Case Road, and then turn right on Perris Boulevard. Turn right at the Ramona Expressway and continue to Lake Perris Drive. The lake, with ten miles of shoreline, invites boaters to sail out to Alessandro Island, named for the Indian hero in Helen Hunt Jackson's *Ramona*. When it was built in 1972, Lake Perris was the southern terminus of the California State Water Project's chain of lakes and aqueducts that brings Feather River water down from Lake Oroville north of Sacramento. Besides sailing, waterskiing, fishing, and swimming, Lake Perris offers spectacular rock climbing and, in season, an area for small-game hunting.

To return home, I-215 is a fast connection to points throughout Southern California.

In the Area

Mission San Juan Capistrano, Camino Capistrano and Ortega Highway, San Juan Capistrano, CA 92068. 714-248-2049.

San Juan Capistrano Historical Society, 31831 Los Rios Street, San Juan Capistrano, CA 92068. 714-493-8444.

Rio Grande Bar & Grill, 26701 Verdugo, San Juan Capistrano, CA 92692. 714-496-8181.

El Adobe Restaurant, 31891 Camino, San Juan Capistrano, CA 92675. 714-493-1163.

Ronald W. Caspers Wilderness Park, 33401 Ortega Highway, San Juan Capistrano, CA 92675. 714-834-2400.

Lookout Roadhouse Restaurant, 32107 Ortega Highway, Lake Elsinore, CA 92530. 909-678-9010.

Crescent Bath House/The Chimes, 201 West Graham, Lake Elsinore, CA 92530. 909-674-3456.

Lake Elsinore Chamber of Commerce, 132 West Graham Avenue, Lake Elsinore, CA 92530. 909-674-2577.

Orange Empire Railway Museum, 2201 South A Street, Perris, CA 92572. 909-657-2605.

Perris Valley Airport, Perris, CA 92572. 909-657-3904.

Lake Perris Recreational Area, 17801 Lake Perris Drive, Perris, CA 92572. 909-657-9000.

4 ~

Clowns of the Desert

Through Joshua Tree National Park

Getting Started: Take the State 62 exit off I-10 north of Palm Springs.

Route: From the West Entrance Station of the Joshua Tree National Park, this route goes through the park to the Cottonwood Springs exit off I-10 east of Indio. About 100 miles.

Highlights: *Tour the bewitching kingdom of the Joshua tree. Get two deserts for the price of one as the higher-altitude Mojave drops down to meet the arid Colorado midway through the park. Watch world-class rock climbers, tour a pioneer homestead, linger in a cool fan palm oasis, and stand on a bluff that overlooks Mexico.*

When driving along State 62 from I-10, the fastest way to get into the park is from the town of Joshua Tree. Turn right on Park Boulevard to the West Entrance Station. The visitors center is at the main entrance at Twentynine Palms fifteen miles farther along the highway, but the scenic route is through the park. Pick up a map from the ranger at the gatehouse and notice how the road you're on loops through the Mojave Desert portion of the park and another angled road runs south through the Colorado Desert.

For the first ten miles through this desert garden, the clownlike Joshuas hold out their awkward bottle-brush arms like novice ballerinas. The Mormon pioneers who came through in the 1850s gave the tree its name because they thought it looked like the prophet Joshua pointing the way to heaven.

These giant yuccas, members of the lily family, sport foot-long creamy blossoms in spring. They thrive only above 3,000 feet in the Mojave Desert portion of the park (park terrain goes from 1,000 to 5,000 feet), so don't be surprised when they disappear as you enter the lower Colorado Desert.

The Park Service has made turnouts along the road. Narrow footpaths lead into the desert, where, if you stand still and watch, you may glimpse the wildlife that hides under the brush—a darting lizard, a leaping jackrabbit, a lumbering giant tortoise, or a scurrying roadrunner. The exotic bighorn sheep and wily bobcats stick to the hills and are hard to spot, but you might catch sight of a coyote out for a kill.

Be sure to stop at Hidden Valley to watch the climbers. Beyond the campgrounds lie twelve square miles of crags and spires, rounded boulders, and walls so sheer they could have been sliced by a mason's saw. Technical climbers from all over the world come here to train in the clear, mild desert air. Telltale ropes dangle down the elephantine boulders along the roadside. Follow them with your eyes to spot the climbers inching their way up the rock faces as their pals critique from below. Rangers have officially recorded more than 4,500 climbing routes throughout the park, rated in degree of difficulty from 5.0, the easiest, to the all-but-impossible 5.14.

Before the park was made a national monument in 1936 (it became a national park in 1994), the grasslands of the higher altitudes, watered by runoff and groundwater, were cattle country. For a while, Hidden Valley was a hideout for rustlers carrying on a stolen cattle trade between California and Arizona. They rebranded their illicit stock and stashed it in this natural corral. A short hike from the picnic area and some scrambling over low boulders will take you to the rock-rimmed

Mormon pioneers gave the Joshua tree its name because they felt it mimicked Joshua pointing the way to the Promised Land

Hidden Valley itself. Across the road, behind the campgrounds, is the start of an easy walk to Barker Dam. Along the way, you'll see some of the park's finest Indian petroglyphs, unfortunately doctored up with paint by a film crew in the 1950s to make the primitive symbols more visible to the camera.

Hidden Valley is also the starting point of a guided walk through a life of the past. On weekends, park rangers conduct two-hour tours of the Desert Queen Ranch, owned by the valley's most resourceful resident, rancher and mine owner Bill Keys, who homesteaded here for more than fifty years until his death in 1969. The Keys family home from 1917 is here, as well as outbuildings, a barn, farm machinery, irrigated gardens, and even a small community schoolhouse. You'll see what it took for a family with five children to make a life in this beautiful but isolated valley.

If the day is clear, don't pass up the six-mile detour to Keys View. Take the Keys View turnoff at Cap Rock Wye, running through Lost Horse Valley. Watch for an informational plaque on the left. It tells the tale of ill-fated cowboy Johnny Lang, who struck gold nearby in the 1890s while searching for a horse that had wandered away from his ranch in Indio. He prospered for a while but ended up a hermit down on his luck and died here while going for supplies. Bill Keys, who came upon the body while digging this road, buried Lang on the spot. His grave is across the road from the plaque.

You can reach the remains of Lang's Lost Horse Mine from here over a rough mile-long dirt road followed by a two-mile hike. Like the 2,000 other mining and prospecting sites that have been found within the park, it was abandoned when the gold petered out. Prospectors who worked the Dale Valley in the rugged Pinto Mountains north of the park had better luck. At one time, there may have been as many as 3,000 people living in the makeshift town that sprang up around one of the Dale mines.

The road to Keys View ends in a big parking lot at the foot of some stairs leading to a vantage point over the Morongo and Coachella Valleys. On a good day, you can see Signal Peak in Mexico ninety-five miles away. One sweep of the eye takes in the lowest and highest points in Southern California. The long, shallow Salton Sea, 225 feet below sea level, is way down to the left, and on the far right 11,485-foot Mount San Gorgonio stands out across the valley.

Now drive back to the start of the detour and turn right to Jumbo Rocks. First in line is gigantic Split Rock. Follow the short trail around to the three-story vertical crevice and natural caves blackened by the cooking fires of Indians and campers. Half a mile farther along is Skull Rock. Its eerie eye sockets are products of centuries of wind and rain that have twisted and cleaved so much of the monument's granite into a fantastic sculpture park.

If you have a four-wheel-drive vehicle you might take a couple of hours for the eighteen-mile self-guided geology tour that starts about two miles along. Brochures describing the natural sights at sixteen turnouts are available at the entrance to the dirt road.

Now that you've seen the Mojave portion of the park, take a break at the visitors center at the Twentynine Palms oasis. For centuries, this shady spring-fed oasis has been a godsend to Indians, pioneers, prospectors, explorers, and hikers who have passed this way.

Turn left at Pinto Wye beyond Jumbo Rocks. Drive past the park boundary and keep going 3.5 miles straight downhill. The visitors center is outside the park, on land donated by the owners of the 29 Palms Inn, whose garden adjoins the oasis. A pleasant park staff will answer questions, and you can find a wide selection of books on desert ecology. Picnic in the shade of a ramada that stretches across the back of the building, or make the short run down to Twentynine Palms Highway for a choice of fast-food places or more gracious dining at the Split Rock Café.

The Serrano Indians called this grove of fifty-foot Washingtonia fan palms the Oasis of Mara, "land of little waters," but the change of name evolved after a survey party came through in 1855 and counted exactly twenty-nine palms—which have, of course, increased since then. One of five such lush refuges in the park, it is fed by water bubbling through natural faults in the rock to fill the pool and nurture the trees and birds.

From the visitors center, reenter the park and continue south past the Pinto Wye turnoff for your descent to the awesome sandscape of the low-lying Colorado Desert. As the clownlike Joshua trees begin to thin out and the vegetation flattens to ground cover, you'll be going through the transition zone between the two deserts. The altitude drops below 3,000 feet as you drive into the drab Pinto Basin. The Joshuas are gone. On your left stand the desolate Pinto Mountains, striated with the brown, rust, and black gneiss that gives them their name.

A river ran through this barren basin 100,000 years ago. Archaeologists say that Pinto Man lived along its green banks hunting camels and saber-toothed cats. Today the land is covered with dusty green creosote bushes, blue-gray smoke trees, and many varieties of eccentric cacti that have made their peace with the parsimony of Mother Nature. The parched land gets only four inches of rainfall a year.

One of the park's most popular attractions is a cactus patch of several acres known as the Cholla Cactus Garden. Be sure to pick up a pamphlet from the box at the entrance to the trail. It will help you identify the jumping cholla, the calico cactus, the jojoba, and other plants whose water-storing bodies and spines allow them to thrive in the desert.

So appealingly fuzzy that one of its names is the teddy-bear cholla, the jumping cholla will stick and wound you at the briefest encounter. Its barbed spines burrow right through your clothing. As you draw back from its sting, a thorny chunk snaps off, leaving the broken barrel impaled in your flesh. In a similar manner, chollas hitchhike on the hides and snouts of feckless animals to be carried far afield, where they can send down new roots. Experienced desert hikers carry pliers or a pocket comb to free themselves from the teddy-bear cholla.

From the garden, the road plunges down past hazy seas of dusty creosote bushes to a thick stand of tall ocotillos, whose sticklike branches sprout delicate scarlet blossoms in the spring. The odd little trees with the grass-green trunks standing along the dry washes are paloverde ("green-stick") bushes. In spring they flower in glorious yellow. The road runs down to the third park entrance at the modest Cottonwood Visitor Center, near the campground at Cottonwood Springs oasis. From the center, it is seven miles through the rock-and-scrub-covered Cottonwood Canyon to I-10 east of Indio.

In the Area

Joshua Tree National Park, 74485 National Monument Drive, Twentynine Palms, CA 92277. 619-367-7511.

29 Palms Inn, 73950 Inn Avenue, Twentynine Palms, CA 92277. 619-367-3505.

Split Rock Cafe, 73502 Twentynine Palms Highway, Twentynine Palms, CA 92277. 619-367-2131.

Twentynine Palms Chamber of Commerce, 6136 Adobe Road, Twentynine Palms, CA 92277. 619-367-3445.

5 ~

Pines to Palms

From Hemet to Idyllwild to Palm Desert

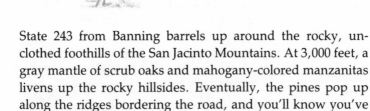

Getting Started: Take I-10 to the Eighth Street exit at Banning.

Route: Take State 243 from Banning to Idyllwild, then State 74 to Palm Desert. About seventy-five miles.

Highlights: *Watch the change from roadside scrub to towering pines as you climb to the charming mile-high town of Idyllwild. Hike the woods, make the rounds of the shops and cafés, or doze under a tree. Stay over in a cozy bed and breakfast. In winter, play in the snow and sit by the fire. Go for a joy ride from pines to palms as the road plunges to the desert floor.*

State 243 from Banning barrels up around the rocky, unclothed foothills of the San Jacinto Mountains. At 3,000 feet, a gray mantle of scrub oaks and mahogany-colored manzanitas livens up the rocky hillsides. Eventually, the pines pop up along the ridges bordering the road, and you'll know you've reached 5,000 feet.

It was the conifer-covered heights that attracted first loggers and then gold prospectors to this part of San Bernardino National Forest in the late 1800s. Later, as word of its dry, clear air spread, tuberculosis patients came to take the cure at sanatoriums that sprang up at Strawberry Valley, the forerunner of the town of Idyllwild. Strawberry Valley's name was changed in 1899 when the wife of a sanatorium manager suggested Idyllwild for the newly built post office.

Your first stop is at tiny creek-fed Lake Fulmor, named for the county surveyor who laid out the highway. You won't see the lake from the road, but turn into the parking lot on the right and chat with the fishermen clustered around their vans. Then walk across the road to the bridge for your first look at this bountiful fishing hole. It's kept well stocked with trout except when the lake freezes over in winter. Take the path around the two-acre lake, then settle in for a picnic.

A half mile up the road, a spectacular panorama spreads out before you at the Indian Vista Point turnout. A Forest Service marker tells you what's what as you look out at the Hemet Valley and San Jacinto Mountains, then over to Cleveland National Forest and Angeles National Forest. On a clear day, you can even make out the dome of Palomar Observatory. If you're there on a day when a gray inversion layer fills the valley, you'll see the view that many Idyllwilders rave about. It's a scene out of a Japanese print, with mountain peaks floating above a sea of mist. On a sad note, Indian Vista Point made world news in the spring of 1994 when two German tourists were attacked and shot, one fatally, in a holdup as they looked out at the view. The viewing point is completely hidden from the road by huge boulders, so make sure there are plenty of other people around before you enter.

From Indian Vista Point, it is about ten miles through the forest to the town of Idyllwild. Before air-conditioning was widespread, Idyllwild was the summer home of people from Palm Springs and the neighboring desert communities. Everyone who could afford it built a cabin among the trees. Today, besides the refugees from the desert, Idyllwild has a sizable year-round population, including a serious artists' colony.

Just before you come to the town, you'll see a sign for the Idyllwild County Park Nature Center. Its exhibits on local flora and fauna, as well as the region's Indian history, are worth the visit, but the highlights are the wildflower garden and the broad deck where you can watch the birds, from jays to hummingbirds, come to the feeders. The half-mile Yellow Pine Forest Nature Trail will whet your appetite for alpine adventure.

One mountain town can be just like another, but Idyllwild, right down the hill from the nature center, revels in its backwoods image. True, businesses have moved from rickety country stores to the Fort, a spanking-new two-story shopping center in the middle of town, but even the Fort has flavor. Whimsical chain-saw art animals stand on the roof. They fit right in with the Tree Monument a block up on Village Center Drive. Since the day in late 1989 when the fifty-foot totem pole, which is also adorned with mountain animals, was unveiled, it has been the most photographed attraction in town. Last time we passed by, a tourist dad was taking pictures of his boys high-fiving Indian Chief Algoot, who stands at the base. The figure lounging behind the chief is Idyllwild's former newspaperman Ernie Maxwell, who mapped out many of the local trails. The crudely painted monument was the work of Idyllwild chain-saw artist Jonathan LaBenne. When the town's oldest resident, a 400-year-old ponderosa pine, was being eaten by beetles, LaBenne rescued it from the woodpile and gave Idyllwild its Eiffel Tower.

There are enough shops and art galleries in town to keep you busy all afternoon. For help with shopping, dining, and lodging and a good town map, drop in at the Chamber of Commerce. It's in the Toys, Wood 'N' Dreams shop on the ground floor of the Fort. The owner carves many of the toys he carries. Other noteworthy Fort shops include Feats of Clay for Indian art and the Reflections gallery of glass. Timber

Ridge, on North Circle Drive, has environmentally correct gifts by inventive local artists. When you're hungry, just walk along North Circle Drive and its little side streets. Jan's Red Kettle is a popular gathering place for light lunches. Pastries by Kathi, a bakery-restaurant, is down the street. A good place for soup and sandwiches is Chelsea's, on Village Lane.

For outdoor information, stop at the U.S. Forest Service's ranger station at the entrance to town or the Mount San Jacinto State Park Ranger Station across from it. Both can give you suggestions for short hikes and beautiful picnic spots.

The southwest corner of the vast Mount San Jacinto State Park Wilderness Area is close to the village. A strong hiker can get to Palm Springs on foot across magnificent but difficult terrain. An eight-mile trail starting from Humber Park near town ends at the top of the Palm Springs tram on Mount San Jacinto.

The campus of the Idyllwild School of Music and the Arts (ISOMATA) at Strawberry Creek is a pleasant stop. You'll see the school entrance at the end of Tollgate Road off State 243 on your way out of the village. Drive in to catch an art exhibit, hear the tones of a flute wafting up from behind a rock, or watch a dance troupe practicing under the pines. Summer programs with as many as sixty different workshops in the arts are tailored for all ages, from kids to Elderhostel groups. In winter, ISOMATA is a private high school for the visual arts.

To start down from the pines of Idyllwild to the palms of Palm Desert in the Coachella Valley, follow State 243 and turn left (east) on State 74. The road unexpectedly turns sharply up over Keen Camp Summit, where the oak-covered mountains echoed with the thunder of horses' hooves in Hollywood westerns in the 1930s. Finally, the road begins to drop down into Garner Valley, named for the 7,000-acre ranch the Garners bought here in 1904. Garner ranch cattle still graze peacefully in green pastures that run for miles on both sides of the road. At the head of the valley is the mountain-rimmed Lake Hemet, a man-made lake from 1895. A mile and a half long and a half mile wide, it is by far the biggest lake in the San Jacinto Mountains. It's too bad that the fishermen's trailer and tenting grounds, enclosed by ugly wire fencing, obscure the beauty of the near shore from the road. To get a real sense of the lake's unspoiled charms, continue on the road running around it or stop for a picnic along the water (no swimming allowed).

Peaceful as the scene is now, the Garner Valley had its hectic moments during the height of gold fever around 1900. But the gold strike and the boisterous village that sprang up with it were short-lived, and the mines rusted away. The Kenworthy Ranger Station near the end of the valley is named for the big Kenworthy Mine.

At the end of Garner Valley, the road heads east across Santa Rosa Summit, then north and downward with increasing drama. Mild scrub-covered desert hills give way to the harsher scenery of parched mountainsides and deep moonscape canyons. Be sure to stop at the viewing point at the top of Seven Level Hill before attacking the hair-raising switchbacks that drop into the Coachella Valley. The descent ends at Palm Desert between Indio and Palm Springs. I-10 and connecting points will get you home.

In the Area

Idyllwild County Park Nature Center, Box 341, Idyllwild, CA 92549. 909-659-3850.

Idyllwild Chamber of Commerce, 25980 Highway 243, Idyllwild, CA 92549. 909-659-8525.

Idyllwild School of Music and the Arts (ISOMATA), 52500 Temecula Road, Idyllwild, CA 92549. 909-659-2171.

Jan's Red Kettle, 54220 North Circle Drive, Idyllwild, CA 92549. 909-659-4063.

Chelsea's, Village Lane, Idyllwild, CA 92549. 909-659-4540.

Pastries by Kathi, 54360 North Circle Drive, Idyllwild, CA 92549. 909-659-4359.

Creekstone Inn, 54950 Pine Crest Avenue, Idyllwild, CA 92549. 909-659-3342.

Strawberry Creek Inn, 26370 Highway 243, Idyllwild, CA 92549. 909-659-2657 or 800-262-8969.

6 ~

A Road That Bears Fruit

From Yucaipa to Oak Glen, Cherry Valley, and Beaumont

Getting Started: Take the Yucaipa exit off I-10.

Route: From Yucaipa Boulevard, turn onto Oak Glen Road, which becomes Beaumont Avenue. Follow it to the town of Beaumont. About twenty miles.

Highlights: *Follow rustic Oak Glen Road past flourishing apple orchards, apple barns, and more than forty charming shops and down-home eateries. Visit the jewel-like Edward-Dean Museum of Decorative Arts and continue on to cherry and antique country. Go in late winter and in spring for cherry and apple blossoms, in June for cherries, in summer and fall for apples, and in winter for shopping and hot cider. It might even snow.*

Start the day at the small foothill town of Yucaipa in a broad agricultural valley east of Redlands in southern San Bernardino County. From the Yucaipa exit off I-10, turn east on Yucaipa Boulevard and left (north) on Oak Glen Road. In about four miles, you'll see the entrance to impeccably manicured Yucaipa Regional Park. On a hot day, it's an inviting place for a swim in a one-acre lagoon with two 350-foot water slides and sandy beaches. You'll also find three small lakes stocked with trout and catfish for shoreline anglers.

At this point, Oak Glen Road is a sedate suburban street, but it soon turns into a gently rolling two-lane road climbing west along the foothills of the San Bernardino Mountains. The rural mailboxes get farther and farther apart, and a big red apple sign welcomes you to the glen.

At one time the whole Yucaipa Valley was dotted with apple orchards, but many growers went under, and most disappeared during the Great Depression. "The cooler the weather, the redder the apple" is the apple grower's credo. Mountain-bound Oak Glen, whose 5,000-foot altitude and snowy winters produced the best red Rome Beauties, an early Yucaipa specialty, survived to become a tourist mecca, attracting as many as a million apple fanciers yearly to its bountiful orchards, brimming farm stands, and quaint country shops.

The man who started it all was a freight hauler from Salt Lake City, Utah, named Enoch Parrish, who, on his regular route to San Bernardino in the 1860s, was struck by the rich mineral quality of the soil and the area's abundant water (Yucaipa is a Cahuilla Indian word meaning "wetland"). The first crop he put in was potatoes; he was so successful that others followed his lead and the little mountain valley became known as Potato Canyon. A year later, he planted the first apple orchard.

Now owned by Joe and Bette Buckle, who used to stop for apples here themselves, the 104-acre Parrish Pioneer Ranch is easy to spot on your left shortly after you've entered the world of green hillsides crosshatched with spreading apple trees and brambly vines of pick-your-own raspberry farms. Turn in past the picnic tables under the towering shade trees and drive up to the old apple ranch, which is now a tiny shopping complex complete with a country-and-western singer, a gunslinger show, and a small animal farm.

On a small rise in the shade of an 80-year-old giant sequoia is the 130-year-old two-story house where the nine Parrish children were born. Across the driveway is the cool, dim adobe-and-oak packinghouse, which is no longer used for shipping since all Oak Glen apples are now sold right out of the ranch farm stands. Remodeled some years ago without losing its old-time flavor, this huge emporium stretches apple marketing to the limit. Row after row of apple cider, apple butter, apple candies, apple jelly, apple T-shirts, apple Santas, apple gifts for teacher, apple wines, and much more line the shelves. There's a bonbon counter and a snack counter as well.

But the crisp, fragrant apples steal the show. Big baskets and bags of just-picked fruit stand at the front of the store. Thirteen varieties are grown on the Parrish ranch, ripening in succession through the season. The Jonathans, Gravensteins, Fujis, and Galas ripen in August, followed by the Spartans, Red Delicious, and Rome Beauties, and so on until the beginning of November. If you're there in September, they'll be picking a Parrish exclusive, the sweet-tart Vasquez apple, developed by Juan Vasquez, who has been the ranch foreman for fifty years. Apple Dumplins Restaurant & Bakery on the premises turns out good country cooking year-round, including a delectable dumpling lavished with a red cinnamon sauce from a recipe from the gone-but-not-forgotten Red Barn restaurant in the Glen.

From Parrish Pioneer Ranch, the road climbs past apple stands and barns, cider mills, eateries, and shops. When the fruit is ripe, a few ranches will open their fragrant orchards for pick-your-own customers—watch for the signs—at about half the price of ready-picked fruit. A stop at Law's Coffee Shop and apple stand introduces you to another Oak Glen pioneer family. Apple Annie's Restaurant & Bakery in Oak Tree Village serves up apple-blueberry and apple-pecan pies, along with French crumb and traditional double-crust apple. A cluster of curio, gift, handicraft, and candy shops surrounds the restaurant for interesting browsing. In a curve on the hill, you'll see the old horse-drawn wagon in front of Los Rios apple barn on the right side of the road. This largest of all the orchards produces twenty-nine different varieties on its 150 acres. Hitch a ride on the wagon for a turn around the ranch.

President Calvin Coolidge's portrait has the place of honor in the 1927 Oak Glen Schoolhouse Museum

As the road makes its way down toward Cherry Valley, you'll see a charming legacy of life in the apple-growing heyday—the two-story stone schoolhouse built in 1927. Its lectern, potbellied stove, and photograph of President Calvin Coolidge glowering from the wall give an eloquent picture of early school days in this idyllic spot. You'll recognize the family names of many of the apple farms you've visited along the way when you inspect the old photos of past classes on the schoolroom wall.

From here the road loses 2,000 feet in elevation as it runs down toward Cherry Valley, home of the Cherry Valley—Beaumont Cherry Festival. At the entrance to the valley is a surprising cultural treat. Watch for the sign to the Edward-Dean Museum of Decorative Arts. The entrance is on your right at 9401 Oak Glen Road. If you're wondering how this rare collection of seventeenth-, eighteenth-, and nineteenth-century art and antiques came to rest in such an out-of-the-way place, it's because two Los Angeles antique dealers had their weekend home here and fell in love with the oak-and-pine-shaded countryside. J. Edward Eberle and Dean W. Stout bequeathed their eclectic collection and sixteen-acre country property for the establishment of this intimate museum and gardens, which opened in 1957. The collection of fine furniture, paintings, sculptures, Persian rugs, and other objets d'art, such as an eight-armed eighteenth-century Waterford chandelier and a group of Italian creche figures, are used to furnish eight period rooms through which visitors are free to wander. The museum is open Tuesday through Friday, 1:00 to 4:30 P.M., and weekends, 10:00 A.M. to 4:30 P.M. It is closed for the month of August.

The two best times to see Cherry Valley are when the trees are clothed in white blossoms in February and at cherry-picking time, from Memorial Day through the third week in June, and some years through the Fourth of July. Plums and peaches ripen in neighboring orchards, which put up signs inviting picking throughout August.

When the cherries are ripe, all of the area's twenty-some ranches open their gates for picking the shiny Bings and Royal Annes. The Cherry Growers Association hands out orchard maps from its booth on the corner of Beaumont and Cherry Avenues, which comes up shortly after Oak Glen Road becomes Beaumont Avenue.

The rest of the year, you are on your own if you want to tour the trees basking in the sun, which the Chamber of Commerce assures us shines more than 300 days a year. One beautiful short loop into cherry land takes you left toward the mountains on Orchard Avenue. The road leads up to Avenida San Timoteo and back on Avenida Maravilla to the highway.

It's great if you can make it for the annual Cherry Festival, usually the first weekend (Wednesday through Sunday), in June. If the temperamental gems ripen on schedule, you can grab a bucket and take to the orchards to eat and pick. The farmer will weigh your buckets and charge you at wholesale prices. In recent years, the festival, held at Beaumont's Stewart Park at Eighth Street and Orange Avenue, has attracted 30,000 people a year. A far cry from its humble inception in 1919, it has grown into a full-fledged fair with cherry royalty, a gala parade, a cherry pancake breakfast, carnival rides, food and craft booths, and pop music stars.

During cherry-picking season, Marilyn's Cake and Catering, which turns out three-pound cherry pies, stays open seven days a week (at other times, just Thursday through Sunday). You can buy a pie or have a slice on the patio with a fifteen-cent cup of coffee. Her record is 400 pies in one day. Look for the pink house at 10218 Beaumont Avenue.

Beaumont's growing antique business makes the trip worthwhile year-round. Beaumont and California Avenues at Sixth Street downtown form a virtual antique mall with around ten places to look through vintage clothing, old glassware, Orientalia, furniture, paintings, lamps, porcelain, and other antiques and collectibles. The Beaumont Antique Bazaar, at 990 Beaumont Avenue and Tenth Street, has an old-fashioned soda fountain. K & M Choice Collectibles is known for its baseball cards.

From Beaumont, you can pick up I-10 only a few miles east of Yucaipa, where you started.

In the Area

Yucaipa Regional Park, 33900 Oak Glen Road, Yucaipa, CA 92399. 909-790-3127.

Parrish Pioneer Ranch, 38561 Oak Glen Road, Oak Glen, CA 92399. 909-797-1753.

Los Rios Ranch, 39610 Oak Glen Road, Oak Glen, CA 92399. 909-797-1005.

Apple Annie's Restaurant & Bakery, 38480 Oak Glen Road, Oak Glen, CA 92399. 909-797-7371.

Oak Glen School House Museum, Oak Glen Road, Oak Glen, CA 92399. 909-797-9691.

Edward-Dean Museum of Decorative Arts, 9401 Oak Glen Road, Cherry Valley, CA 92223. 909-845-2626.

Marilyn's Cake and Catering, 10218 Beaumont Avenue, Cherry Valley, CA 92223. 909-845-1767.

Beaumont–Cherry Valley Cherry Festival Information: Beaumont Chamber of Commerce, 450 East Fourth Street, Beaumont, CA 92223. 909-845-9541.

7 ~

Cruising the Rim

From San Bernardino to Lake Arrowhead and Big Bear Lake

Getting Started: Take I-10 to I-215 in San Bernardino.

Route: From San Bernardino, take I-215 north to State 30 to State 18 (Rim of the World Drive). Follow this route to Lake Arrowhead and Big Bear Lake. From there, take State 38 to Redlands. About ninety miles.

Highlights: *Visit glamorous Lake Arrowhead and rustic Big Bear Lake; catch a future Olympic skating star training in Blue Jay. Shop Lake Arrowhead Village. Take a lake cruise. Ride the chair-lift to the top of Snow Summit. Follow the Holcomb Valley Gold Fever Trail. Stay overnight at Lake Arrowhead or Big Bear Lake. You may hate yourself later if you just drive through.*

The Rim of the World Drive is a pleasure all the way, but getting to it means negotiating a tangle of turns if you're coming from I-10 in San Bernardino. From I-10, take I-215 north to State 30 and exit at Waterman Avenue (State 18). This will launch you on the Rim of the World Drive, which is actually State 18. Just beyond the hillside homes of San Bernardino, you'll whiz past the turnoff to Waterman Canyon. The Serrano Indians built their villages along the steaming hot springs within the canyon's protective walls. Later it was the home of the elegant Arrowhead Springs Hotel, where the crème de la crème came to take the waters. On the hill behind it, a seven-acre natural rock formation in the shape of an arrowhead points straight down to the site of the old spa. (You can see it clearly from Waterman Avenue in San Bernardino.)

The road climbs swiftly past brush-and-yucca-covered hills, which can be dazzling in spring when the brilliant golden Spanish broom is out. When the Rim of the World Drive reaches 4,000 feet, it turns east to skim along the brink of the mountain toward Lake Arrowhead and Big Bear Lake. You can look back at the zigzag road and imagine the pioneeer Mormon lumbermen of the 1850s struggling up a cruder version of this route in ox-drawn wagons on their way to Mormon Springs. That's now the town of Crestline just over the ridge.

About six miles down the Rim of the World Drive, just after you pass Rimforest, turn left on Daley Canyon Road (which becomes State 189). It leads to Lake Arrowhead's unpretentious little suburb of Blue Jay. Named for the raucous Steller's jays that share the pines with chickadees and woodpeckers, Blue Jay has come into its own as a figure-skating capital with the establishment of the Ice Castle International Training Center here. You never know when you'll bump into Olympic gold medalists Irina Rodnina, who coaches here, and Robin Cousins, the center's director, or any number of familiar skating stars.

Blue Jay has had a skating rink for at least fifty years. The first one was a small patch of melting ice where the Thrifty drugstore is now. One of the little girls who skated there on hot summer days, up to her blades in water, was Carol Caverly, who went on to become an Ice Follies star. In 1982, she and her husband, Walter Probst, built the training center, which now attracts serious skaters from more than twenty countries. Part of the project is the Olympic-size public Ice Castle Skating Rink, with canvas sides that open to let in the forest. It's the long barnlike structure behind the fairytale drawbridge at the edge of the village. You may see future medalists polishing up some fancy spins and triple lutzes there. But the serious figure-skating training is at the center's hillside campus on a sequestered rink where skaters can check out their form in a mirror that runs the entire width of the rink. It is officially open to the public only for group tours, but once when we showed up alone, a doting skating mother invited us to watch the practice. To reach this rink and the training campus in the woods, continue on State 189 to a sharp curve in the road. You'll see Cottage Grove Road coming in almost straight ahead. Take it and make an immediate right onto Burnt Mill Road.

When you return to the main road, you'll be just around the corner from Lake Arrowhead Village. As you pass the flagpoles of the luxurious Lake Arrowhead Resort, you'll see sapphire Lake Arrowhead, ringed by mansions with private canopied docks, each, it seems, with a ski boat tied to it. Behind the houses is a wall of black-green ponderosa, sugar, and Coulter pines. We like to pass up the first entrance to the village and go farther down to the lakefront. Having to take a four-story elevator ride down a concrete parking structure adds nothing to the mountain experience.

Today's bustling Bavarian village was built from scratch in 1979 after the old Tudor-style buildings were razed to make room. The only reminder of the good old days, when the town turned out to dance at the pavilion on summer evenings, is an octagonal building with a spire. It now houses boutiques. If you like shopping, this complex of fifty shops offers upscale clothing, gifts, novelties, antiques, sporting goods, furniture, cookware, and sweets.

At last count, you could choose between nine village restaurants, including a McDonald's with a terrace on the lake. At the end of the shopping street, you'll see a gracious waterfront pavilion and emerald lawns for picnics. The lake is privately owned by the property owners in the immediate vicinity. Tourists can't use it for swimming or boating. The only trespasser we've seen recently in the water was a golden retriever eagerly paddling after a flock of mallards.

You can, however, get out on Lake Arrowhead on the little white paddle-wheeler tour boat *Arrowhead Queen*. The fifty-minute tour is a better way to see the architectural details of the lakefront mansions along the 12.5-mile indented shoreline. Driving around the lake can be frustrating because the backs of the houses are to the road. When the captain has finished telling you how Bugsy Siegel kept a gambling casino in his basement, how Howard Hughes used to land his airplane on the lake, and that the old apple orchard nearby was used to feed the stills in the Roaring Twenties, he'll get down to the story of the lake.

Man-made Lake Arrowhead lies in what was once the Little Bear Valley, where lumbering was so intense that at one time the hills were completely stripped. The old sawmills disappeared underwater when a dam was begun in the 1890s for a valley irrigation project that was later abandoned. One of the old sawmills, according to the captain, lies near the base of the blue tower (part of a filtering system) that you see sticking up out of the water. The largest sawmill—train tracks, workers' houses, and all—is at the northeast end, where the newer multimillion-dollar estates of today's CEOs and movie moguls spread along the shore. The homes built by Clark Gable, Bette Davis, Cary Grant, Bing Crosby, and their Hollywood friends, located in the older "Beverly Hills" section of the lake near the village, look like humble lakeside cottages compared to the new ones. At least one mansion has its own inside dock with an electric garage door, and one estate has a river running through the grounds. Just about anyone who wants one has an electric tram to get from the house to the dock.

Beyond the lake is beautiful and varied country. Lake Arrowhead's mountains stood in successfully for Switzerland in Shirley Temple's *Heidi* and for Florida's piney woods in *The Yearling* with Jane Wyman and Gregory Peck. At the ranger station on State 18, just east of the village, you can pick up a trail map that will lead you into the fragrant forest. For a beautiful walk of only two-thirds mile, take the Heaps Peak Arboretum Trail, starting a couple of miles down the road from Santa's Village (see next paragraph). It is particularly gorgeous in May, as is all of Lake Arrowhead, when clouds of creamy dogwood blossoms are spread beneath a dark canopy of giant sequoias. The Pacific dogwood is rare in Southern California, but it thrives in the Lake Arrowhead microclimate. The town has a big dogwood parade and festival at the height of the blossoms in mid-May.

When you're ready to push on, follow State 173 out of the village lot past the elegant Tudor-style Saddleback Inn (left over from the good old days) to Kuffel Canyon Road. Turn left onto State 18 for a stretch of spectacular valley views from the Rim of the World Drive. If you have toddlers, they'll make you stop at bubble-gum-pink Santa's Village two miles down the road. The old gent and his elves are there all year, and the kiddies can feed the reindeer, ride the ponies, and go on the candy-cane sleigh, giant bumblebee monorail, merry-go-round, and other little tots' rides. A puppet show and a raft of shops selling toys, cookies, and souvenirs can hold a family captive for several hours.

About seven miles farther down the highway, after you've passed the start of the Heaps Peak Arboretum Trail, you'll see State 330 coming up to Running Springs from Redlands. You'll know by Running Springs' faded ski rental signs, which nobody bothers to take down in summer, that you've entered another world. From here on in, the mountains belong to the fishermen, boaters, hikers, skiers, rock climbers, and bikers. Three major ski areas—Snow Valley, six miles ahead, Snow Summit, and Bear Mountain rising 6,754 feet above Big Bear Lake—operate throughout the winter, sometimes by the grace of high-powered snowmaking machines.

At Snow Valley, coming up on your right after the snow-tubing hill, thousands of skiers and snowboarders hot-dog down the snowy slopes, which reach an elevation of 7,852 feet at Slide Peak. You can see the bunny hills from the road, but the warm-weather Green Valley Trail affords a sweeping view of the heights. It starts across the road from the parking lot.

From Snow Valley, the Rim of the World Drive twists up twelve miles to Big Bear Lake. When you come to the dam, stay to the right on State 18. You'll want to tour the popular south shore first.

Big Bear Lake is nine miles long and four times bigger than Lake Arrowhead. It was built to water the citrus groves and farms in Redlands down the hill, but the idea was

Sailing on Lake Arrowhead

abandoned ages ago. This part of the mountains shares a common history with Lake Arrowhead, except for the short but sweet gold rush of 1860 in the Holcomb Valley over the hill to the north. Prospecting fever brought a flood of 2,000 people, including the legendary Lucky Baldwin, who struck it rich at his Gold Mountain Mine. The farms of Bear Valley grew food and provided lumber for the new mining towns before the dam that filled up Bear Valley was built in 1864. The lake was promptly stocked with fish from Lake Tahoe, and it has been a favorite of trout and bass fishermen ever since.

Some of the wooden houses near the end of the lake stand on government lease land and were built on grade to preserve the natural contours of the land. By law, their exteriors cannot be changed and the colors must be the browns and greens of the forest. Some were built for the men who worked on the dam. The "Chinese" house on its own island just offshore was the home of the engineer who masterminded the dam. The low, green-roofed houses have kept the west banks of Big Bear Lake as natural as it must have looked a century ago. You'll see more of that look at Boulder Bay, next along the road. This jumbled bay with houses anchored into the rocks is a picture best seen from on high. Take the half-mile hike (fairly steep) that leaves from the road a little way back toward the dam. Look for the sign to the Castle Rock Trail.

The road has recently been routed under the wooden welcome arch and straight into Big Bear Village. The new Northwoods Resort on your left is Big Bear's first big hotel, opened in late 1994. Its duck pond becomes a skating pond in winter. The handsome lodge is right in step with Big Bear's march away from the log cabin look to a new Alpine image. Many of the old stores damaged in the Landers Earthquake of 1992 have come back as chalets, and purple and red petunias brighten the streets. If you're looking for a good informal place to eat after doing the antique stores, try Boo Bear's Den on Pine Knot Avenue.

For a guide to restaurants, inns, sports, and Big Bear's big festival schedule, drop in at the Chamber of Commerce at 630 Bartlett Road in the heart of the village. The big celebration here is the Oktoberfest, held on weekends in September and October at the Convention Center at the east end of the lake. It's a nonstop German beerbash, with brass bands, dancing, Bavarian food, and folks in lederhosen.

Unlike Lake Arrowhead's closed-in shores, Big Bear's are easy to tour by car, but you'll probably want to get out among the water-skiers, and sailboats, windsurfers, and fishermen on this breezy, inviting lake. You can rent a boat from one of eight marinas along the road or take the *Big Bear Queen* tour boat from Big Bear Marina—if you're in the mood to listen to another captain's spiel.

The mountain-biking craze has taken over the Snow Summit ski area. In winter, the mountain at the head of Summit Boulevard is a Grandma Moses landscape come to life, with bright spots of color in motion on the sparkling snow. A few years ago, the treeless ski hill was deserted in summer. Now helmeted bikers crowd around the lift waiting for a ride to the top. The bikes ride with them, dangling from stout iron hooks. Take a round-trip ride to the Summit Haus deck, elevation 8,200 feet, and watch the hotshot bikers take off down the old logging roads. The restaurant looks south into the San Gorgonio Wilderness, in the opposite direction from the lake.

Tucked into a canyon at the lake's east end is the Bear Mountain ski resort, where high-speed lifts take skiers 8,440 feet up Gold Mine Mountain for a two-mile run, long for these mountains. There's nothing doing there off-season, but across from the ski lodge is the Moonridge Animal Park, where you can see injured forest animals being rehabilitated for release back into the wild. Sometimes there's even a bald eagle that couldn't keep up with the flock of some thirty birds that regularly migrate to the lake. To get to the park, turn right off the highway on Moonridge Drive and follow the signs to the ski area.

To see the wilder side of the lake, backtrack on State 18 to the Stanfield Cutoff and turn left on State 38 on the other side. You'll find long stretches of empty shoreline, some waterfront campgrounds, boat launch facilities, picnic areas, and places to walk by the water or look for beavers among the willows along the edge. Fishermen cast their lines from the sandy banks or wade in to bow-fish for crappies. The best views are from this side as well. California's tallest peak, 11,499-foot Mount San Gorgonio, slants up across the lake behind the local mountains. The treeless runs of Bear Mountain, on the far left, and Snow Summit, on the right, are spread out in miniature from here.

The north shore is the jumping-off point for a drive into the wild Holcomb Valley. The ranger station two miles east of the Stanfield Cutoff will give you a Gold Fever Trail map. The twenty-mile trail, over good dirt roads, takes about three hours and leads to the rich gold-mining territory discovered by prospector Bill Holcomb, who struck it rich one day in 1860 while he was out hunting grizzlies. You'll see the remains of boomtown Belleville, Hangman's Tree, and the Lucky Baldwin Mine, among the few tangible memories left from those days.

As you continue along the lake, you'll want to know that the building floating in the water is the S.S. Relief, the rest room-on-a-dock for the convenience of boaters. And the silver-domed observatory on the narrow causeway that runs out in the lake is Caltech's Solar Observatory for tracking solar flares. As locals won't let you forget, Big Bear Lake was chosen for these studies because of its clear skies and perpetual—330 days per year—sunshine. The observatory gives tours on Saturdays from 2:00 to 4:00 P.M. during July and August.

The last part of the road runs through the small town of Fawnskin and past hillside cabins until it comes back to the dam. To go back down the valley, you have a choice. The shorter way is to return to Running Springs on State 18 and take State 330 to Redlands. You also can get to Redlands through Barton Flats, as many Big Bear Lake people do.

Go back along State 18 to the east end of the lake past Moonridge Drive and the service town of Big Bear City. Turn right on State 38, and you're off on your way over 8,443-foot Onyx Summit. You'll come practically face-to-face with Mount San Gorgonio's snow shoulders and drive through a steep, thickly forested canyon and down to the popular Barton Flats campgrounds. When you come out of the trees, you'll pass Mill Creek, in summer a bone-dry river of rocks with the sweep of an Alaskan glacier. At the end of the road lies Redlands and I-10.

In the Area

Ice Castle Skating Rink, 27307 Highway 189, Blue Jay, CA 92317. 909-336-1111; Training Center: 909-337-0802.

Lake Arrowhead Chamber of Commerce, Vineyard Bank Building, Lake Arrowhead Village, Lake Arrowhead, CA 92352. 909-337-3715.

Lake Arrowhead Resort, 27984 Highway 189, Lake Arrowhead, CA 92352. 909-336-1511.

Saddleback Inn, State 173, Lake Arrowhead Village, CA 92352. 909-336-3571.

Snow Valley Ski Resort, Box 2337, Running Springs, CA 92382. 909-867-5151.

Big Bear Chamber of Commerce, 630 Bartlett Road, Big Bear Lake, CA 92315. 909-866-7000.

Snow Summit Ski Resort, Box 77, Big Bear Lake, CA 92315. 909-866-5766.

Bear Mountain Ski Resort, 43101 Goldmine Drive, Big Bear Lake, CA 92315. 909-585-2519.

Big Bear Marina, Big Bear Lake, CA 92315. 909-866-3218.

Pleasure Point Marina, Big Bear Lake, CA 92315. 909-866-2455.

Pine Knot Marina, Big Bear Lake, CA 92315. 909-866-2628.

Boo Bear's Den, 572 Pine Knot Avenue, Big Bear Lake, CA 92315. 909-866-2932.

Northwoods Resort, 40650 Village Drive, Big Bear Lake, CA 92315. 800-866-3121.

The Knickerbocker Mansion Bed and Breakfast, 869 South Knickerbocker, Big Bear Lake, CA 92315. 909-866-8221.

8 ~

Canyon Country

From Newhall to San Francisquito and Bouquet Canyons

Getting Started: From the Los Angeles area, take I-5 to State 14, then take the San Fernando Road exit off State 14.

Route: Follow San Fernando Road to Newhall. From there, take San Francisquito Canyon Road up San Francisquito Canyon to the Leona Valley. Follow Bouquet Canyon Road to Valencia Boulevard. About fifty miles.

Highlights: *Visit the ranch of silent-screen cowboy William S. Hart. Search for the St. Francis Dam. Load up at the bountiful Leona Valley farm stands and return down rustic Bouquet Canyon. Count on at least half a day, longer if you hike or dawdle. Work in some fun at Six Flags Magic Mountain amusement park in Valencia.*

Start at the San Fernando Road exit off State 14. Follow San Fernando Road west 1.7 miles into Newhall, and as soon as you cross the railroad tracks, turn left at the unmarked gate of the William S. Hart Regional Park. (For some unknown reason, the big sign with the saddle comes *after* you've passed the gate.)

Although few people today remember William S. Hart, "Two Gun Bill" was the cowboy king of the westerns in the silent-movie days. He and his Hollywood posses thundered across the Santa Clarita Valley in more than sixty shoot-'em-ups from 1914 to 1925. After his final movie, *Tumbleweeds,* he retired to the 265-acre Horseshoe Ranch, which he had used as the set for many of his films. He built a twenty-room Spanish Colonial mansion, La Loma de los Vientos (Hill of the Winds), overlooking the range he used to ride.

"While I was making pictures," Hart said, "the people gave me their nickels, dimes and quarters. When I am gone, I want them to have my home." When he died in 1946, he left his ranch to his fans.

The short, steep path on the right of the parking lot leads up to his two-story white ranch, now a county museum with docents waiting at the door to walk you through. Long before he faced the cameras, Hart had been fascinated by Indian cultures and cowboy lore. He was a stickler for authenticity in his pictures and collected the finest Navajo rugs, Indian baskets, cowboy trappings, antique firearms, paintings, and sculptures, including works by Frederic Remington and Charles Russell. Hart filled his comfortable home with these treasures. He also filled it with his Hollywood pals. Robert Taylor, Barbara Stanwyck, Will Rogers, and Maurice Chevalier frequently hid out here from their adoring publics. However, Hart always reserved one bedroom for his two man-size harlequin Great Danes, which are buried in the dog cemetery out back.

If you've brought youngsters, they'll enjoy the collection of barnyard animals and the small herd of bison in the corrals at the bottom of the hill. The property's original little ranch house also is open, with Hart's movie memorabilia on display. And if you feel like hiking, a network of trails leads through gentle terrain in the ranch's backcountry. The grounds are open daily. House tours are offered Wednesday through Sunday.

Before moving on, take a look at the yellow wooden 1876 Saugus Train Station and the historic engines next door. Just walk through the side gate near where you drove in. The station did some traveling itself, when the Santa Clarita His-

William S. Hart left his ranch home to the County of Los Angeles as a museum

torical Society, now headquartered in the station, saved it from destruction after the Southern Pacific Railroad discontinued passenger service in Saugus. It was cut apart and trucked down San Fernando Road from Saugus three miles away. The waiting room, with its wooden floor and Franklin stove, is open on weekend afternoons only, looking much as it did when the stationmaster and his family lived upstairs and crowds of people from Los Angeles would get off the train bound for a rodeo or a day of hunting.

One thing missing from the old days is Tolefree's Saugus Eating House, which opened in the station in 1887. It later moved directly across the street from the depot, and it is still open as the twenty-four-hour Saugus Café. Amid a funky red-checkered decor with fascinating old photos on the walls, you can get anything from old-fashioned chicken-fried steak to trendy fajitas. After leaving the Hart ranch, you'll pass it three miles down San Fernando Road at the corner of Drayton.

Turn left out of the ranch and continue on San Fernando Road, which veers into Bouquet Canyon Road, then left again on Seco Canyon Road into San Francisquito ("San Fran") Canyon. If you've seen the view from the 284-foot Sky Tower at Magic Mountain, you know how quickly the manicured suburbs disappear into the creases of the San Gabriel Mountains, rising 2,000 feet to farm and ranch country along County N2, which runs to Palmdale on the east and I-5 near Gorman on the west.

The steep natural pathways were used by the Tataviam Indians on their way to their hunting grounds. Later came gold seekers, stagecoaches, celluloid cowboys, and the water and power company that built the ill-fated dam.

The St. Francis Dam disaster was second in California only to the San Francisco Earthquake in loss of lives and property. The place where the dam burst more than half a century ago has since been disguised by man and nature, but you can find the remains if you know where to look.

At San Francisquito Canyon Road, turn left into the wide mouth of the canyon, past the grazing cattle, "No Prospecting" signs, and off-road-vehicle trails and up through chaparral-covered hills to the Forest Service station. Stop and set your mileage counter back to zero for the trip to the elusive site.

The towering hydroelectric plant just behind the Forest Service station is known as Power Plant 2. It was rebuilt after its predecessor was swept away in the blink of an eye one night in March 1928. This plant and Power Plant 1, seven miles up the canyon, were the sole suppliers of Los Angeles's electricity at the time. The St. Francis Dam, upstream from the plant, was a project of William Mulholland, the eminent manager of the municipal water and power company and considered the father of L.A.'s water and power system. The dam had been up for less than two years when the 185-foot concrete wall collapsed, sending a giant wave thundering down the canyon, toppling Power Plant 2, and sweeping away people, animals, houses, and trees all the way to Newhall. When it hit the bed of the Santa Clara River, it followed the river to the ocean near Ventura, wiping out broad swathes of the towns of Piru, Fillmore, and Santa Paula on the way. An estimated 450 people were killed, and more than a thousand homes were destroyed. Mulholland, who had inspected the dam and pronounced it safe that very day, resigned from his post as manager of the water and power department, his illustrious fifty-year career in shambles.

There is no sign pointing to the dam site; old-timers say that officials have always tried to cover up this disgrace. Most cars zip right past this powerful piece of history and never see it, but you will if you keep your eye on your mileage counter. At mile 1 from the Forest Service station, you will see a broad plateau on the left littered with what looks like a jumble of white rocks. Many of them are actually chunks of concrete swept down from the dam, but the dam itself is on your side of the road. At mile 1.5, pull into the one-car parking spot just before the curve in the road. Pick your way up the roadside embankment, and you'll be looking straight down at the wall of infamy. The huge rock pile on your right, with its mantle of dirt and grass, is actually the dynamited remains of a piece of the dam wall that didn't collapse. If you look closely, you'll see twisted strands of telltale rebar sticking out from the "rocks." Down to the left is an unusual sight in this dry canyon—a dense green forest of cottonwood trees, lush even in the driest August. They are growing in the dam's lake bed, watered by runoff that is trapped by the rubble.

Although L.A. now gets 90 percent of its electricity from coal-powered plants and other sources, the generators here are still turning, fed by the water rushing through the wide bands of silvery pipe running down the canyon like six-lane highways. Near the top of the canyon, a small sign marks the roadway down to Power Plant 1, which is hidden in a deep hollow on the right.

When the road emerges at the top of San Francisquito Canyon, you'll be on the western edge of the lush Leona Valley. Turn right on Elizabeth Lake Road, as County N2 is called along this stretch. This road was built in a notch in the mountain made by the infamous San Andreas Fault. People with houses and farms along the road don't seem concerned. They point out that no major quake has occurred along the San Andreas Fault in Southern California since the big one in 1857 leveled Fort Tejon near Gorman. Many of the people around here work in Palmdale, fifteen minutes away, but some are gentlemen farmers enjoying the wide-open spaces.

Plans are in the works for an 8,000-acre housing and commercial development at the Palmdale end of the valley. But for now, cherry, Asian pear, and apple orchards still produce delectable pick-your-own crops along the road. Big John Mayfield, a building contractor turned farmer, keeps his stand open all season from the first cherries of June through the peaches, watermelons, corn, tomatoes, and bell peppers of summer and the Asian pears and pumpkins of fall. You'll find his stand in front of his cherry orchard in the little town of Leona, one block below the main road. Turn right at Ninetieth Street West, then right onto Leona Avenue.

Bouquet Canyon Road is just beyond Leona. To go back down the mountain, turn right and cut across the sweep of farmland to the head of the canyon. Although Bouquet is greener than San Francisquito, with stands of bright sycamores and cottonwoods relieving the dark oak, don't expect masses of wildflowers even in spring. Somewhere along the line, a cowpoke twisted Rancho del Buque (*buque* is Spanish for "sailing vessel") into Bouquet. The seductive glimpses of cobalt-blue water that flit in and out as you enter the canyon are of Bouquet Reservoir, a surprising giant, built to store water out of harm's way below the San Andreas Fault. It is not open for recreation. You can, however, get your feet wet (but the ranger warns visitors not to drink) in Bouquet Creek, which trickles a few yards from the road. There's a pleasant place to picnic at Streamside Campground about twelve miles along. If you'd rather enjoy a drink or snack at an umbrella-shaded table on the patio of a hundred-year-old stagecoach tavern, stop at Big Oaks Lodge. On Sunday, the lodge serves barbecue from 11:00 A.M. to 6:00 P.M.

Bouquet Canyon Road ends in a glamorous subdivision at the foot of the hill and connects via Valencia Boulevard to I-5.

In the Area

William S. Hart Regional Park, 24151 San Fernando Road, Newhall, CA 91321. 805-259-0855.

Saugus Train Station, 24107 San Fernando Road, Newhall, CA 91321. 805-254-1275.

Saugus Café, 25861 San Fernando Road, Saugus, CA 91321. 805-259-7886.

Big John's Orchard and Fruit Stand, 9852 Leona Avenue, Leona, CA 93557. 805-270-1735.

Big Oaks Lodge, 33101 Bouquet Canyon, Saugus, CA 91321. 805-296-5656.

Six Flags Magic Mountain, 26101 Magic Mountain Parkway, Valencia, CA 91385. 805-255-4111.

9 ~

Presidential Pomp to Small-Town USA

From Simi Valley to Moorpark, Fillmore, and Lake Piru

Getting Started: From the Los Angeles area, take I-5 to State 118. Follow State 118 to the Madera Road exit in Simi Valley.

Route: From Simi Valley, take State 118 to Moorpark, State 23 north to Fillmore, and State 126 east to Lake Piru. About sixty miles.

Highlights: *Tour the Ronald Reagan Presidential Library in Simi Valley on the western edge of L.A.'s San Fernando Valley. Then follow two-lane roads to the old ranch town of Moorpark and across a rugged canyon to the picturesque town of Fillmore. Drive through the orange groves to hidden Lake Piru.*

You'll find yourself at the west end of the Simi Valley, called Shimiji by the Chumash Indians who built their rush dwellings here 8,000 to 10,000 years ago. It remained wilderness, then ranch land until Simi Valley became a bedroom community for Los Angeles in the 1960s and was incorporated as a city. The opening of the Ronald Reagan Presidential Library here in 1991 brought Simi Valley into the national limelight. Like the other 160,000 visitors per year, you'll be making your way south along Madera Road and turning in at Presidential Drive. The library stands at the end of a sweeping road lined with slender young eucalyptus trees. The red-tile-roofed mission-style building holds 23,000 feet of cases filled with 50 million pages and 1.5 million photographs.

Visitors can watch a film on the Reagan years and call up significant events in history on interactive video machines. As you wander through the display areas, you'll see a changing selection from the more than 75,000 gifts of jewelry, statuary, paintings, furniture, and antiques that the Reagans received from world dignitaries while they were in the White House. An exact replica of the Oval Office and the First Lady's Gallery seem to get the most attention from tourists. Be sure to go out to the garden in back with its panoramic view of brush-covered mountains. There you'll find a section of the toppled Berlin Wall with pink butterfly graffiti. The library is open daily Monday through Saturday from 10:00 A.M. to 5:00 P.M. and Sunday from noon to 5:00 P.M.

When you leave, turn left on Madera Road, then left at the bottom of the hill on Tierra Rejada Road. Through a fence on the right, you can glimpse the Strathearn Historical Park and Museum, a collection of buildings including the Simi Adobe from the late 1800s and the set for the TV show *Little House on the Prairie*. The park is open Saturday and Sunday from 1:00 to 4:00 P.M. The entrance is behind the K-Mart store on Strathearn Place. If it happens to be Sunday, you can check out the "junque" at the teeming 125-stall swap meet that overflows the parking area of the Simi Valley Drive-in coming up immediately on the right.

From here the road turns rural for a modest stretch, with palomino horses and black-and-white cows peering over ranch fences. Then the houses spawned by the growing community of Moorpark take over. Turn right on Los Angeles Avenue and left on Moorpark Avenue, then right on High Street, shaded by wispy pepper trees. This is Moorpark's "old town," a slice of life revolving around the coming and going of the trains. The yellow station at the entrance is not the old depot but a false front put up to hide the silos of a feed mill behind it. That's really the only hokey touch. The clothing store in the old service station, once one of the only places to fuel up between Ventura and the San Fernando Valley, still has the gas station facade.

The Castro Grocery looks exactly as it did sixty years ago—except for the capuccino sign in the window (et tu Moorpark?). It's now The Creamery, an ice cream parlor serving forties-style banana splits and root beer floats (and vegetable croissants) while the jukebox spins out Glenn Miller. The proprietor will give you a printed walking tour guide to the twenties and thirties houses in the neighborhood. You can find your own way among the antiques and collectibles in the shops along High Street.

If you favor biscuits and gravy with your breakfast steak, a good stop for chow is the Cactus Patch on High Street. This homey coffee shop is the "in" spot, filled with cowboy mementos and black-and-white photos of Hollywood stars, many of whom have ranches here.

Apricot orchards built the wealth of early Moorpark families. In fact, the town takes its name from a popular apricot variety. These days, the land is covered with citrus groves, and since the early 1950s Moorpark has been one of the biggest egg producers in the country.

You'll see both when you go back down High Street and turn right on State 23 toward Fillmore. Dry hills dotted with cacti suddenly change to orange groves protected by stands of towering eucalyptus trees, the windbreak of choice in Southern California. If the air seems perfumed by other than orange blossoms, you can blame it on the seemingly never-ending rows of gray-slatted chicken coops coming up on your left at Egg City and the Embly Ranch. More than a million chickens are housed here, producing eggs four or five times a week.

Turn left at the Embly sign onto Shekell Road. The egg producers are not tourist attractions, but this little roller-coaster road will lead you past glorious orange groves and a small slice of Moorpark's horse country. Where Shekell Road ends at Broadway (an unlikely name for this bucolic lane), turn left and then right on Grimes Canyon Road for a drive past green pastures.

Behind one stretch of white fence is Hales and Horses Polo Farm, at 7916 Grimes Canyon Road. Owner Sally Hale says she was one of the first women in the United States to compete in polo (she disguised herself as a boy). She and her two daughters, who followed in her footsteps, put on matches at their own emerald-green polo field here on Sunday afternoon and Thursday night during the summer. The public is welcome, but phone ahead.

Follow your tracks back to State 23 for a wake-up ride between the steep walls of Grimes Canyon. Fillmore teenagers used to take driving lessons on this tortuous road. Oil rigs once sprouted like trees from the hills above. Grimes Canyon was part of the rich oil-producing area from Castaic to Saticoy. You can see a few remaining towers, but the boom has passed, and the hills are now used for mineral quarries.

The road down to the valley leads past small farms with rabbits and oranges for sale, then goes over the old-fashioned green bridge that spans the sluggish Santa Clara River to Fillmore. At Telegraph Road (State 126), turn right and go four blocks, then turn left on Central Avenue to the center of town.

Founded in the late 1880s as a Southern Pacific Railroad town, Fillmore was a favorite movie location because of its small-town look until the January 1994 Northridge Earthquake wiped out 117 mobile homes, 80 houses, and 14 businesses, including the historic movie theater where Fillmore residents saw their first talkies. Plans to start filming *The Young Indiana Jones Chronicles* the morning of the earthquake were cut short. Scaffolds soon enveloped the injured downtown buildings of mortar and unreinforced brick, and the area has been remodeled without ruining the "set."

Be sure to visit the antique stores along High Street in Moorpark

Fillmore's 1880s train depot, now a local history museum, and a collection of old locomotives came through the quake with no problem and are fun to inspect. A drive through the compact residential section of town takes you past beautiful old homes that survived the quake. The elaborate redwood Episcopal Church at Second and Saratoga Streets, with its unusual lych-gate to hold a bier, was used in the opening scenes of *The Thornbirds*.

Back at State 126, turn left, heading east for the twelve-mile ride to Lake Piru. A highway sign along this stretch of road instructs you to turn on your lights during the day for added safety. Don't forget to turn them off when you stop at the farm stands that line the route with vegetables for sale straight from the fields. Everything grows in this fertile valley—corn, berries, avocados, nuts, lettuce, tomatoes, celery, broccoli, pumpkins, and squash, depending on the season. But the prizewinners are the navel oranges as big as grapefruit in winter and the unrivaled juicy Valencias as the spring sets in. If you can't decide which stand to pull up to, watch for Cornejo's on the right at the edge of a grove. The pickers dump the oranges into the sorting machines right by the vegetable bins, while hens with their chicks get underfoot.

Now get ready for a right turn onto Fish Hatchery Road, which runs between a rhubarb farm and a watercress farm to the trout-raising ponds of the Fillmore State Fish Hatchery. Protective netting keeps out the birds. You can read about the breeding and growing process on the bulletin board and put a nickel in the fish food dispenser. This is a must stop if you've brought the kids.

It's about four miles farther to the turnoff for the town of Piru. Just after the state highway sign announcing Piru in one mile, look for an unobtrusive country road called Main Street on the left. It leads you past the packinghouses of the Fillmore-Piru Citrus Association and through a town of 1920s bungalows where camera crews are frequent visitors. You saw Piru in Faye Dunaway's TV film *Silhouette,* and the plane crash in Dustin Hoffman's *Hero* was shot at the town bridge.

Main Street soon turns into rural Piru Canyon Road. The small stream running down toward you is on its way to the Santa Clara River. The road climbs six miles through meadow covered with scrub oak and brush. A few minutes after your first glimpse of 200-foot-high Santa Felicia Dam, you'll be at the entrance to the Lake Piru Recreation Area, at the foot of the pine-covered Los Padres National Forest, a good place to picnic, hike, or boat. Under the sparkling blue waters of the lake, which was formed when the canyon was flooded in 1955, are layers of history, beginning with artifacts from the Indians whose word for the reeds from which they wove their baskets was *piru.* Some historians believe that a cache of gold, known only to the Indians who hunted here, lies under the waters. And old-timers still talk about the one-room Temescal Joint Union School now buried beneath the water as well.

Today the four-mile-long lake, bordered by campgrounds, comes alive with boaters, swimmers, water-skiers, and fishermen in search of rainbow trout, bass, bluegills, and catfish. Cougars, black-tailed deer, bears, raccoons, opossums, and foxes roam the gentle hills of this protected wilderness. Ospreys and golden eagles patrol the skies above the lake.

On the way back down the road from Lake Piru, stop at the hand-lettered sign on the right that says "Honeycomb" and drive through the gate. Two scruffy, brindled Queensland heelers lounged in front of the small house under a giant elm tree the day we stopped. Beekeeper Ann Bennett greets customers on her screened porch at a table laden with jars of pure honey—sage, orange, wildflower, and avocado. Honeycombs and small jars of bee pollen, good for allergies and extra energy, she says, also are for sale. Next to them stands the cash register, a coffee can decorated with yellow paper and with a slot in the lid. Mrs. Bennett doesn't bother to look while customers deposit their money.

Ann and her husband, Red, who quit a city career in aerospace for the isolation of Piru Canyon more than fifteen years ago, maintain one of only five beekeeping operations in Ventura County. The hives are in back of the house, 1,000 two-story boxes with a colony each, 40,000 bees to a colony. Go out and look at them in winter when the bees are inactive, but in summer watch out! The bees are apt to be flying around. You can make good time getting home by retracing your steps through Piru to State 126 east, which connects to I-5.

In the Area

Ronald Reagan Presidential Library, 40 Presidential Drive, Simi Valley, CA 93065. 805-522-8444.

Strathearn Historical Park and Museum, 137 Strathearn Place, Simi Valley, CA 93065. 805-526-6453.

Moorpark Chamber of Commerce, 530 Moorpark Avenue, Moorpark, CA 93021. 805-529-0322.

The Creamery, 255 High Street, Moorpark, CA 93021. 805-529-0417.

Cactus Patch, 1097 High Street, Moorpark, CA 93021. 805-529-9550.

Hales and Horses Polo Farm, 7916 Grimes Canyon Road, Moorpark, CA 93021. 805-529-9572

Fillmore Chamber of Commerce, 344 Central Avenue, Fillmore, CA 93015. 805-524-0351.

Lake Piru Recreation Area, 4780 Piru Canyon Road, Piru, CA 93040. 805-521-1231.

Bennett's Honey Farm, Box 175, Piru Canyon Road, Piru, CA 93040. 800-521-2889.

10 ~

The Midas Touch

From Placerita Canyon to Lancaster and Tropico

Getting Started: From the Los Angeles area, take I-5 to State 14, then take the Placerita Canyon Road exit near Newhall.

Route: From Placerita Canyon Road, take the Sierra Highway to Rosamond. About eighty miles.

Highlights: *See the place where gold was first discovered in California in 1842, at Placerita Canyon. Explore the incredible Vazquez Rocks, where movie moguls turned Hollywood westerns into gold. In spring, plan a detour to the incredible Antelope Valley California Poppy Reserve. See the rare leopards and tigers at the Exotic Feline Breeding Compound in the shadow of the abandoned Tropico Mine.*

Winding Placerita Canyon Road leads to the Placerita Canyon Nature Center, guardian of the Oak of the Golden Dream, where the first gold strike was made. There's more gold in "them there hills," but a sign on the gate says "Gold Mining Including Hand Panning Is Prohibited."

No one knows for sure why rancher Francisco Lopez and two companions happened to ride into this particular meadow one spring afternoon in 1842 or why Don Francisco singled out a particular oak to lean against for his siesta. But so the story goes, he dreamed he was swimming in a pool of gold. Later he happened to dig up a bunch of wild onions nearby, and having done some prospecting in his time, he recognized a promising glint in the sand that clung to the roots. Records are in short supply, but after the word got out, at least 1,000 pounds of gold dust and small nuggets were dredged and sifted out of Placerita Canyon dirt before the local miners joined the stampede to Sutter's Mill in 1848.

Near the far end of the entrance to the park's visitors center, a short path leads under the highway to a grassy meadow where the Oak of the Golden Dream still stands. Only a low wooden fence protects it.

The cabin across from the parking lot is the old Walker place. Frank Walker, his wife, Hortense, and their twelve children lived in the ten-by-twenty-foot house in the 1920s. Although the gold was pretty much played out by then, Walker regularly augmented his farming income by a few dollars' worth of placer deposits. If the cabin looks familiar, it's probably because it's been in dozens of films, as has every inch of Placerita Canyon. Producers love unspoiled country that lies within Hollywood's sacred thirty-mile zone. This is the longest distance that crews are willing to go on location for a day without being lodged overnight at studio expense.

When you've finished exploring, continue on Placerita Canyon Road, then turn left on Sand Canyon Road. Turn right on the Sierra Highway. With the Antelope Valley Freeway (State 14) taking the brunt of the traffic, this old road can afford to amble through ranch land and mining country until it gets to urban Palmdale.

You're headed for Vasquez Rocks County Park, which is probably the only park in the country named after a bandit who was hanged. Turn right onto Aqua Dulce Canyon Road and follow it for about two miles, past the comfortable homes and green pastures of affluent horse-breeding country. Turn left on Escondido Canyon Road. Rising in front of you will be some of the most photographed rocks in the world—the

150-foot canted Vasquez Rocks, leaning like golden sails in a sandy sea.

This hogback ridge (the geological term) was formed by ancient layers of solidified sand folded and tilted at angles as sharp as fifty degrees over 25 million to 40 million years. Riddled with caves and crannies, it was the hideout of the well-born gentleman bandit Tiburcio Vasquez and his desperadoes, who rustled cattle, stole horses, and highjacked stagecoaches up and down California during the 1850s and 1860s. Their intricate fortress baffled and repulsed all pursuers. The lawmen might never have caught Vasquez if he hadn't taken up with the wife of one of his own men. The outraged husband betrayed Vasquez to the sheriff, and Vasquez was wounded in the ensuing fight. Nevertheless, Vasquez outran the pursuing posse and escaped to nearby Soledad Canyon, hiding out with a price on his head until he was captured and hanged in 1875.

The play *Bandido!* by Luis Valdez, which premiered in Los Angeles in 1994, draws a complex picture of the outlaw as a Latin Robin Hood. The dapper Vasquez took from the rich and gave to the poor. He justified his crimes as a protest against the Yankees who swarmed into California during the gold rush of 1848 and stayed to take over the land.

The end of Vasquez wasn't the end of shootouts at Vasquez Rocks. Hollywood discovered this ready-made stage set in the 1920s, and the rocks have been featured in hundreds of westerns and straight adventure films from *The Charge of the Light Brigade* to *Maverick*.

The rocks also doubled as the moonscape for *Star Trek* and as the habitat of *The Flintstones of Bedrock*. They have helped sell millions of dollars' worth of products in TV commercials. According to the park ranger, filming goes on at least four times a week—remember the thirty-mile rule. While we talked with the ranger, eager scouts from two studios showed up, clipboards in hand.

When you can tear yourself away from this spectacular place, double back to the Sierra Highway. You'll soon start a gentle climb toward the old railroad and mining town of Acton. Mines such as the Red Rover and Governor wrested millions of dollars' worth of gold and silver from those dusty tan hills to the north beginning in the 1880s.

Acton is a good place to find a restaurant. Besides the fast-food places along the road, there's the 49er Saloon, a popular spot for lunch and dinner. To get there, turn right down Crown Valley Road, and go two miles. You'll see the Old West facade on your left, behind the Antelope Valley Bank.

The Sierra Highway continues its gentle rise along the edge of the hills. Then it drops on down to Palmdale. Palmdale stands at the southern entrance to the Antelope Valley, followed by Lancaster and Rosamond, the latter a neighbor to Edwards Air Force Base, which lies seventeen miles east of Rosamond along two vast dry lakes.

Palmdale's sea of red-tiled roofs is a legacy of the 1980s, when the three aerospace towns were booming. Palmdale's population alone quadrupled. On the right side of the road is U.S. Air Force Plant 42, a complex of major government contractors. The first buildings rising out of the desert floor are part of the Lockheed Corporation. Rockwell International, in the same lineup, turns out space shuttles for NASA and retrofits them after touchdown.

If you're here in the spring, you'll see enchanting bursts of wildflowers all along this route. But they're only a preview of the glorious orange hills at the Antelope Valley California Poppy Reserve in Lancaster. The reserve is usually open mid-March through May. Call ahead to make sure the finicky flowers are out in enough numbers to make the thirteen-mile drive worthwhile. Some years, when the rainfall is not to the poppies' liking, the reserve may open later in the year or close earlier.

Drive through the town of Palmdale and turn left (west) onto Avenue I for the ride out to the poppy show. You'll have to endure some industrial scenery and the treeless California State Prison simmering in the sun, but a reward is coming as Avenue I becomes countrified Lancaster Road and delivers you to the gateway to the golden carpet. Drive in through the gate and around to the visitors center, built into the hillside. A wall of dual-pane glass allows the sun to heat the building while giving visitors a panoramic view of the fields.

California poppies spread some gold

The center has good botanical exhibits and pamphlets on the eight different varieties of poppies here, as well as the thousands of different wildflower varieties around the state. Surrounding the building are inviting trails that loop around the flowering hills. You can drive or walk them before backtracking to the Sierra Highway.

Every year on a weekend in mid-April, Lancaster holds its poppy festival at the city park at Avenue L and Tenth Road West, featuring a magnificent flower show and a carnival. Shuttle buses take you out to the reserve, where you can take a hot-air balloon or helicopter over the poppy fields. For information, contact Lancaster City Hall.

As the Sierra Highway continues, small clumps of Joshua trees appear along the road, relieving the monotony of the chaparral. Preservationists raised a storm of protest over the destruction of these grotesque giants when developers bulldozed them left and right during the Antelope Valley's building boom. The trees, which are actually overgrown relatives of the yucca and members of the lily family, are rarely seen outside the deserts of Southern California, Utah, Arizona, and Nevada. The city of Palmdale now requires builders to preserve at least two Joshuas per acre, and Lancaster is raising money to protect its dwindling wooded areas.

When you get to Rosamond Boulevard, turn left and continue for about three miles. At dusty Mojave Tropico Road, turn right and follow the sign to the Exotic Feline Breeding Compound. It's at the foot of the hill littered with shacks from the abandoned Tropico Mine.

In this desolate stretch of desert, California big-cat fanciers Joe and Jeannie Maynard established a refuge for the preservation of wild felines that are being crowded out of their natural habitats throughout the world. Joe, a retired trucking executive, developed an interest in animals during his boyhood in the wide-open spaces of the Saugus-Newhall area before World War II. Later, in the 1960s, before private ownership of wild animals was forbidden, he bought a leopard from a newspaper ad, and his interest developed from there.

The compound, a nonprofit corporation, works on cooperative breeding programs with zoos and universities throughout the country. Methods such as in vitro fertilization, embryo transplants, and cryopreservation of sperm and ova are part of the ongoing research.

The compound is home to about fifty cats, including nine northern Chinese leopards, the largest captive breeding population at one facility in the world. There's also a male Amur leopard; fewer than one hundred such leopards are still in the wild. For a small donation to support the animals, visitors get a forty-minute guided tour by a trained docent. You can see most of the animals, provided they're not sleeping inside their dens. The big crowd pleaser is Southeast Asia's white-striped fishing cat. In the wild, he uses his partially webbed furry toes to swim out into lakes and rivers. Tours are given daily, except Wednesday, from 10:00 A.M. to 4:00 P.M., but according to director Maynard, the best tour is the last one, at 3:30 P.M. That's when the cats come out of their lairs to pace up and down before dinner. They are fed after closing.

On the way out, you can view the Tropico Mine, where gold was found in the late 1890s, through the locked fence. At its zenith, this mine was the queen of the Antelope Valley. It operated until the mid 1950s. The International Chili Society took advantage of this Old West setting for its annual chili cook-off until the early 1980s.

For the drive home, State 14 is an efficient alternative to the Sierra Highway.

In the Area

Placerita Canyon Nature Center, 19152 Placerita Canyon Road, Newhall, CA 91321. 805-259-7721.

Vasquez Rocks County Park, 10700 West Escondido Canyon Road, Saugus, CA 91350. 805-268-0840.

49er Saloon, 31908 Crown Valley Road, Acton, CA. 805-269-1360.

Antelope Valley California Poppy Reserve, 5101 West Lancaster Road, Lancaster, CA 93536. 805-724-1180.

Lancaster City Hall, 44339 Fern Avenue, Lancaster, CA 93534. 805-723-6077.

Exotic Feline Breeding Compound, Rhyolite Road, Rosamond, CA 93560. 805-256-3332.

11 ~

Ghost Towns Living or Not

From Mojave to Randsburg to Calico

Getting Started: From I-5 near Los Angeles, take State 14 to Mojave.

Route: From Mojave, take State 14 north to Red Rock Canyon. Then double back on State 14 to Randsburg Junction. Take Redrock-Randsburg Road and Garlock Road to Garlock. Return to Redrock-Randsburg Road and follow it east to Randsburg. Take US 395 to State 50 east. In Barstow, take I-15 to Yermo and Calico. About eighty miles.

Highlights: *Relive the treasure hunt of the 1880s in the Mojave Desert's fabled ghost towns. Stop at Red Rock Canyon. Follow the trail to the big gold strike at Randsburg and visit Calico. Tour the Calico Early Man Archaeological Site.*

The gigantic forty-mule-team borax wagons that flashed across our TV screens in the opening credits of *Death Valley Days* (actually eighteen mules and two horses) used to end their 165-mile journey through the desert at the railroad terminus of Mojave. Then a big borax strike in nearby Boron put them out to pasture in 1889. Today Mojave makes history of another kind. The *Voyager*, the first nonstop, nonrefueling plane to circle the globe, was designed and built at Mojave Airport. Edwards Air Force Base, the second largest air force base in the United States, and NASA's Dryden Research Facility are just down State 58.

State 14 leads north past a string of boxcars along Mojave's right-of-way that might have seen the mules more than a century ago, then curves sharply to the right to follow the western edge of the mineral-rich sand where men found fortunes in gold and silver that put the borax mines to shame. It is an easy twenty-three miles to Red Rock Canyon, where gold was discovered in 1893 a couple of years before the Mojave Desert's biggest strike at the Yellow Aster Mine in Randsburg. One eye-popping nugget found at Red Rock reportedly brought $2,000. The glowing orange rock canyon also paid off in other ways, yielding rich fossil finds from horses, antelope, mastodons, and rhinoceroses. Today Red Rock Canyon State Park is set up for campers, who come to hike or bike the paths that disappear behind the canyons convoluted walls. Try an exploratory hike of your own, then hop in the car and backtrack down State 14 to the Randsburg Junction. Turn left at the junction; you'll be confronted with a choice of two unmarked roads. Take Redrock-Randsburg Road, the one on the right along the Southern Pacific Railroad tracks. What looks like a streak of snow in the distance is a long mound of salt mined from Koehn Dry Lake.

In about twelve miles, start watching for a narrow road to Garlock on the left. And when you make your turn, don't blink because you'll miss Garlock. For a town with an illustrious mining history, Garlock's two or three falling-down shacks on the side of the road are a disappointment, especially if you've seen photographs of Main Street at the height of its glory. A thousand miners pitched their tents and lean-tos in Garlock in 1893 when gold was discovered in Goler Canyon a short hike to the north. Main Street was lined with shops, saloons, and dance halls ready to show the miners a good time. But they closed down and were left to rot when the miners here heard about the Yellow Aster Mine and followed the pack ten miles to Randsburg.

Return to Redrock-Randsburg Road and follow it east to Randsburg. A lineup of rusty tin-roofed dwellings will lead you to Butte Avenue, the refreshingly unretouched Main Street. To their credit, the 200 hardy folks who live here and love it have resisted the urge to pretty up the place for tourists. Everything in this four-block downtown section needs painting, and dogs sit in the middle of the road.

In its heyday, Randsburg was one of three small mining towns only a couple of miles apart. Red Mountain was known for its saloons, gambling halls, and floozies. Its biggest claim to fame was the rich silver strike at the Kelly Mine in 1918. Johannesburg, called Joburg around here, was planned as a service community for the surrounding mining camps. The streets were laid out in an orderly grid. It even had a golf course and a thirty-three-room hotel with a parlor and bar, which burned down in 1910. Old houses and mobile homes now serve a dwindling population. Neither Joburg nor Red Mountain even came close to matching Randsburg's fame and wealth.

The Yellow Aster bonanza swelled the town to 3,500 people by the turn of the century, when a total of $3 million in gold had been taken out of the ground. That was even before the mining company started crushing the rock with a 100-stamp mill, instead of the 10- or 30-stamp mills it had used before. You can see what a 10-stamp mill looks like in the dusty little town park on Butte Avenue. The park is no great shakes, but it does have convenient rest rooms.

The Yellow Aster Mine has had its ups and downs but is currently operating around the clock. You'll pass it on your way out of town. It is not open to the public.

If you're in luck, someone will be shooting a movie or a music video the day you arrive in Randsburg. You'll think you've stumbled onto the Paramount lot. Guys in Stetsons and gals in bonnets hang out in front of the post office during their breaks or sip lemon phosphates at the marble soda foun-

Stop in Randsburg's White House Saloon, where Death Valley Scotty and Seldom Seen Slim once played poker

tain in the Randsburg General Store, established in 1896. But even if no one is filming, you can get the flavor of the good old days at the general store or the adobe White House Saloon across from the post office. The saloon was opened as a card room in 1903 and was patronized by the likes of Death Valley Scotty and Seldom Seen Slim. The bar where hotheaded miners used to shoot it out on Saturday nights is open all day

Friday through Monday until 6:00 P.M. Sandwiches and chili are served.

Fire has been a constant threat to the flimsy wooden buildings in Randsburg; half the business district burned down in 1898. Among the few structures that were saved are a shed and adjoining rooms that make up Austin's Second Hand Garage across the street from the park. It starts with an open ironworking shed cluttered with tools, bolts, hinges, mining equipment, and auto parts. Next door is the rambling depository for antiques and collectibles. Every available surface is crammed with pressed glass, painted china, old dolls, period clothing, filigree jewelry, and household oddities.

Across the street is the down-home Huss-ee Gift Shop, and next door is the Butterfly Craft Shop, where the proprietor makes crocheted flowers and sews her own doll clothes and quilts. Several of the shop owners here sell their own homemade crafts. If you're in town on a weekend, when the Desert Museum is open from 10:00 A.M. to 5:00 P.M., you can see photos of the good old days and get a grasp of the mining process.

Leave town by following Butte Avenue in the opposite direction from where you entered. The road runs through the newer part of town and then past the Rand Mining Company's Yellow Aster Mine before joining US 395. While you're waiting to make your right turn, have a look at Red Mountain across the road to your left and try to pick out the profile of a miner's face that locals swear they can see when the light is right.

Expect an uneventful ride through the desert to the old railroad town of Barstow, which grew up in the 1880s around the junction of the Southern Pacific and Santa Fe Railroads. Barstow was named for the man who was president of the Santa Fe when his company's tracks were laid, and the city is still an important railroad division point. It's also the only town we've seen where the McDonald's is housed in old railroad cars. To get to Barstow, follow US 395 to State 58 east. As you approach, turn right on Irwin Road, right on First Street, and left on Main Street. Then turn right on Barstow Road and follow it up the hill, making a right on Virginia Way to the Mojave River Valley Museum.

There's always an enlightened volunteer on duty at the museum to enlarge on the extensive exhibits, such as the fossils from the Calico Early Man Archaeological Site, precious Indian pots and baskets, mining and railroad paraphernalia, and information about the valley's present role in space research and military defense.

A set of taillights is a reminder that Barstow was a stop on old Route 66. In the museum's front yard, you can climb into a cowboy train car fitted with bunks, where the men rode on their way home from the cattle drives.

Another stop you might want to fit in is the Calico Early Man Archaeological Site at Yermo (open Wednesday through Sunday until 4:00 P.M.). To visit the dig, return to Barstow Road. Turn right and take I-15 east. Get off on Minneola Road, turn left, and follow the signs along a graded dirt road for 2.5 miles north.

In 1942, an amateur archaeologist stumbled on what looked like chipped stone tools buried on the shores of extinct Lake Manix. The earliest known man-made artifacts in North America were found in this Pleistocene lake, leading scientists to believe that people have been in the New World for 200,000 years. Before that, people were thought to have arrived 10,000 to 20,000 years ago. This dig was the only North American project undertaken by Louis Leakey, who directed the work until his death in 1972. You can walk through the dig on your own or take a guided tour (the last tour is at 3:30 P.M.) and see some of the 9,000 flintlike quartz tools, some still embedded in the walls of the excavations. So far no human bones have been discovered.

From here, head back on I-15 to Calico. Take the Ghost Town Road exit and follow the signs to the parking lot in a narrow canyon. You'll see busloads of tourists from all over the world.

Calico was a rough-and-ready boomtown from 1881 until the early 1890s. Between $60 million and $80 million worth of silver was extracted from the forty-mile Calico mining district, $13 million from Calico Mountain right in back of the town. Then the silver ran out, the miners drifted away, and Calico became a ghost town, its buildings disintegrating under the desert sun.

In the early 1950s, Walter Knott of Knott's Berry Farm in Buena Park bought the town and rebuilt it into a seamless fantasy of old and new. He later donated the reborn ghost to San Bernardino County. We can't think of any other county park with restaurants and shops run by concessionaires who look as if they just stepped off the train from Fargo.

The mix of fantasy and reality starts with a short tram trip up to the town, set on a small plateau among ruddy hills mottled in the earth tones of a calico cat. The town's main street looks like an old photo of itself that's been overly retouched. The "old" houses, which are new, stand on their original foundations. An imitation narrow-gauge railroad runs past the real Silver King Mine. You'll know you've stepped into the past when you jump back to avoid a mock gunfight breaking out in front of the Assay Office.

Near the top of the tram is a diagram that tells you which "hundred-year-old" buildings are new and which, like Joe's Saloon, the R & D Store, and the Lucy Lane House, have genuine remnants of their former selves. Don't miss the boutiques and antique stores, with clerks dressed as ladies and gents and generous reminders of the Old West everywhere. Lucy Lane's back room, for example, has an old miner's kitchen, a dentist's office, and a blacksmith's shop. In the general store, a placard tells of the harsh realities of life in these hills before the town's glamorous remake: "What made Calico run? Wagon wheels, wood and kerosene, beasts of burden and elbow grease made Calico run."

The town stays open until dusk for strollers, but Calico's shops and eateries close at 5:00 P.M. You can still get an old-fashioned malt and a hearty American meal at Peggy Sue's Diner in Yermo. When you come down from Calico, turn right on Ghost Town Road and go under I-15. Turn left on Yermo Road, and you'll see Peggy Sue's on the corner. To get home, I-15 connects with principal roads in all directions.

In the Area

Red Rock Canyon State Park, Cantil, CA 93519. 805-942-0662.

Desert Museum, 161 Butte Avenue, Randsburg, CA 93554. 619-374-2111.

Randsburg General Store, 35 Butte Avenue, Randsburg, CA 93554. 619-374-2418.

Mojave River Valley Museum, 270 East Virginia Way, Barstow, CA 92311. 619-256-5452.

Calico Ghost Town Regional Park, Ghost Town Road, Calico, CA 92398. 619-254-2122.

Calico Early Man Archaeological Site, Minneola Road exit from I-15, Yermo, CA 92398.

Peggy Sue's Diner, Yermo and Ghost Town Roads, Yermo, CA 92398. 619-254-3370.

12 ~

Over the Ridge

From Castaic to Fort Tejon, Hungry Valley, and Pyramid Lake

Getting Started: At Castaic, take the Lake Hughes Road exit off I-5.

Route: From Castaic, take Lake Hughes Road to County N2 toward Gorman. From Gorman, take I-5 north to Fort Tejon, then south to Hungry Valley and Pyramid Lake. About seventy-five miles.

Highlights: *View spectacular Castaic Dam and follow the infamous San Andreas Fault to the Tejon Pass. Visit historic Fort Tejon, ride along with the daredevil off-road vehicles in Hungry Valley, and end at California's new water and power museum at Pyramid Lake. Go in spring for the lupine and poppies. In winter, you can detour from I-5 to 8,800-foot Mount Pinos for Alpine scenery and cross-country skiing.*

Modest Lake Hughes Road starts climbing along the east side of imposing Castaic Lake, a vital link in the chain of dams built by the California State Water Project. Lying in a chevron-shaped canyon, it extends its arms like two gigantic wings with twenty-one miles of shoreline, which also includes a separate lagoon at its base. The near east wing is reserved for sailing and fishing (for bluegills, bass, and trout), while the west wing is a speedway for Jet Skis, water-skiers, and motorboats. For an up-close view of the water, beaches, jogging trails, and picnic places, take the turnoff to the main launch ramp.

From the lake, the road follows an old wagon trail into the Sawtooth Mountain country of the San Gabriels, leaving civilization behind. Shady Ruby Canyon Road, coming in from your right, is a twisting dirt path to neighboring Francisquito Canyon. Don't be tempted to turn down it without a four-wheel drive. Keep climbing and watch the dry yuccas and brush give way to sycamores and pines as you reach the fork at the top of the road. The road ahead is County N2 with local names that change along the way. Turn right on Elizabeth Lake Road (County N2), which runs past Lake Hughes, a private lake that is quite hidden from the road.

At the first crossroads, you'll come to the rambling Rock Inn, built in 1929 of gray river stones to replace an old burned-down roadhouse. If you can squeeze in among the herd of iridescent Harleys parked outside, you'll find a cavernous old tavern with murky stained-glass windows, a battered bar, and a pool table in the middle of the room. This haven for hungry day-trippers and bikers is also the social gathering place for this secluded woodsy neighborhood. On weekend nights, the place vibrates with live rhythm and blues and country music played by musicians holding forth on a makeshift stage near the big stone hearth. Upstairs the inn has a few old-fashioned bed and breakfast rooms for a quick country getaway from Los Angeles.

Up the road about a mile is Elizabeth Lake, ringed by low, nondescript hills and houses but a pleasant place nevertheless. It is administered by the Forest Service and is a popular spot for locals who come to picnic, fish, and swim. Sometimes a stiff breeze brings out the windsurfers, and there's always at least one fisherman on the water. Elizabeth and Hughes are not the typical man-made lakes of Southern California. They are a gift of the San Andreas Fault, which created the saps, or depressions, they fill. Rain and runoff from the mountains keep the water up, except during bad droughts when a small lake like Elizabeth can disappear. The San Andreas Fault runs all the way up from Palmdale, providing a convenient crease in the hills for the road. In fact, when you drive along County N2, you're actually driving right over the fault.

Turn back (if you dare) along County N2 and go straight past where Elizabeth Lake Road changes to Pine Canyon Road. Relax until you reach Three Points. Be on the alert because the road signs show Pine Canyon Road going in three directions. Be sure to follow the one to the left around the ninety-year-old general store. If you continue on the road straight ahead, you'll end up on the floor of the desert at Lancaster.

After the turn, the road shrinks to a sliver. You can idle along enjoying the quail skittering under the oaks and in springtime stop for pick-your-own cherries. Curve after curve brings airplane views of the golden desert as the road makes a steep downward spiral. Then, just when you begin to wonder if you've gone wrong, it turns up abruptly. After a series of sharp S curves, it reaches a dented sign that says "Sandberg." That grand old name, now just a sign on the road, marks the home of the beloved Sandberg Hotel, once the finest hostelry on the two-lane Ridge Route from Castaic to Gorman.

When it opened in 1915, the Ridge Route cut the drive from Los Angeles to Bakersfield to a mere eight hours. But a day's trip along its harrowing switchbacks required frequent rest stops and water for a boiling radiator. Gas stations, roadside cafés, gambling casinos, speakeasies, and hotels like the Sandberg flourished along the way until four-lane Highway 99 went in, cutting the drive to less than four hours.

Highway 99 became history itself in 1972, when I-5 replaced it, cutting the time to two hours. Just after the Sandberg sign, turn right on a short stretch of the historic Ridge Route. If you look to the left before you turn, you'll see the dilapidated road starting its lonely hairpin path back down to Castaic. It's now used mainly by firefighters.

At Highway 138, turn left along the shore of skinny Quail Lake (another earthquake sap along the San Andreas Fault) and turn right on Old Post Road. These rolling hills could be a million miles from nowhere, except for the California Aqueduct cutting a sparkling blue path through the countryside and the grinding and whining of big rigs laboring up I-5 to the top of the 4,100-foot Tejon Pass. Gorman, just around the corner, has been a traveler's haven since stagecoach days. Gorman was named after Private James Gorman, once a soldier at Fort Tejon, who homesteaded several hundred acres in 1864 where the stage stop was established.

Part of the Ralphs Ranch, owned by members of the L.A. supermarket family, this traditional stop for coffee and gas now has a modern motel. A spiffy Carl's Jr. has taken the place of the old lunchroom where the Greyhound bus stopped when Highway 99 ran by. In the spring, Carl's Jr. is a good place to stop for a free wildflower guide. Had you been one of the thousands of tourists who came by in October 1991, you would have seen "flowers" in autumn. The Tejon Pass was a living canvas for the artist Christo, who is known for his monumental outdoor projects. He planted hundreds of big market umbrellas and turned the hills into a huge garden of giant yellow blossoms.

Turn north on I-5 past the turnoff to Frazier Park and Mount Pinos at the top of Tejon Pass. From there it's a short way down to Fort Tejon State Historic Park at Lebec.

Fort Tejon grew out of President Millard Fillmore's attempt to control Indian-pioneer relations. He appointed Edward Fitzgerald Beale, who already knew the California area from his exploits in the Mexican War, to the post of superintendent of Indian affairs for California, and in 1853 Beale established the nation's first Indian reservation, seventeen miles down the hill in the San Joaquin Valley. The fort followed in 1854 to protect both the reservation Indians and the settlers from marauding desert tribes. The first adobes were demolished when the San Andreas Fault caused the great quake of 1857, but the compound was rebuilt and remained in service until 1864. It was the last stop for the camel train that carried supplies across the desert from San Antonio, Texas, in an army experiment with these beasts in 1857. The camels proved intractable and were subsequently sold off.

As you cross the footbridge over narrow Grapevine Creek, the broad, grassy parade ground will be straight ahead. That's where Brigadier General Beale reviewed the U.S. Dragoons of Company A in their sky-blue uniforms and cocked hats. Pick up a pamphlet at the park's small museum before you head out to visit the reconstructed jail, guardhouse, barracks, captain's home, and junior officers quarters, furnished even down to life-size mannequins of the inhabitants. These buildings are only a sample of the forty that stood in this clearing, which stretched past where the freeway is now. Never in danger of military attack, Fort Tejon was built without protective walls and had the look and lifestyle of a well-kept village—the country club of forts, some called it. It is still the most pleasant place to picnic along I-5.

On your rounds, don't miss the old oak tree in a corner of the grounds. An inscription carved in its bark reads: "Peter le Beck, killed by xxx [presumably for grizzly] bear, October 17, 1847." Historians know that beaver trappers from the Hudson's Bay Company settled these parts in the early 1830s, but that's all they know about the man who gave the town of Lebec its name. On the first Sunday of the month year-round, the "Dragoons" come out to re-create life at the fort. From April through October, on the third Sunday of the month, earnest men in blue and gray hold their own maneuvers in the hills. Their Civil War reenactment is not as big a stretch as it sounds, since Dragoons from Fort Tejon were sent to the South in 1861 and nine Fort Tejon officers became Civil War generals.

Across the freeway is what looks like a glamorous private home on a small rise. That's the headquarters of the Tejon Ranch, which covers an area about as big as the city of Los Angeles. What you see from the road is the tip of the iceberg. Behind the mountains, cowboys ride herd on 12,000 head of cattle. Walnut, almond, and pistachio groves and vineyards cover 3,662 acres, and the company also does business in oil and real estate. Most of its 420 square miles that sprawl across the back of the Tehachapi Mountains and into the Antelope and San Joaquin Valleys is land that General Beale amassed during a subsequent career as surveyor general for California and Nevada. In 1912, his son Truxton sold it to a group of Southern California businessmen headed by Harrison Gray Otis, the publisher of the *Los Angeles Times*. It's now a publicly owned corporation.

None of the other Dragoons did nearly as well as their leader. Some of the men, for example, established homesteads in a wide pocket of land called Honey Valley just across the highway from Gorman. The name was eventually changed to Hungry Valley, reflecting the fortunes of the settlers, whose homes have since disappeared.

Take the freeway back to the Gorman exit and turn west, away from town, on Gorman School Road, then immediately right on Peace Valley Road. Backtrack north alongside the freeway for one mile, and a sign will lead you into Hungry Valley.

Hungry Valley is now a State Vehicle Reserve Area of 19,000 acres, the second largest of the state's seven off-road-vehicle parks. Motorcycles, dune buggies, ATVs, and four-wheel-drive vehicles leap up the hills, bump down the ravines, and streak along the sand washes on eighty miles of trails. You'll see plenty of action from the fifteen-mile Gold Hill Road that curves through the reserve. Only half the road is paved, but the dirt section is smooth and safe for passenger cars. If earsplitting motorcycles don't appeal to you, the wildflower show in spring and summer will.

During most of the year, yellow mustard grass provides the color, but in April and May the valley is a wall-to-wall carpet of blooms. Photographers' tripods outnumber ATVs. Finding a place to stop along most highways is a frustrating business, but here you can park on the side of the road almost anywhere and linger as long as you like beside fields of orange poppies, yellow coreopsis, purple lupine, and pink owl's clover. Look closely, and you'll see dozens more varieties. The park rangers, who know their flowers, lead two-hour drive-and-walk caravans to the best viewing places on Saturday and Sunday at 1:00 P.M. For information call Hungry Valley headquarters.

When you leave the valley, turn right on Smokey Bear Road, actually a piece of Highway 99, which runs to the boat ramp at Pyramid Lake and disappears under the waters that buried it when the dam was built in 1973. Pyramid Lake, by the way, stands on land that General Beale once bought for four cents an acre. A right turn on Smokey Bear Road leads to the entrance of the lake, whose twenty-one miles of canyon-lined shore are so remote that most of its beaches are reachable only by boat.

Southern California water sports lovers and fishermen have the State Water Project to thank for dams such as Pyramid and Castaic that give us our recreational waters. Just down I-5 at the Vista del Lago exit, you'll see a palatial Mediterranean villa perched on a promontory over Pyramid Lake. Opened in late 1993, the Vista del Lago Visitors Center uses entertaining displays and a knowledgeable staff with PR savvy to showcase the prodigious network of reservoirs, pumping plants, hydroelectric power plants, aqueducts, and pipelines that bring life to the arid southland. A neon sign in the rotunda sets the stage by inviting you to drink from a fountain of "liquid gold," water that has made the trip all the way from Lake Oroville to the Feather and Sacramento Rivers, through the Sacramento–San Joaquin River Delta, and down the California Aqueduct to Pyramid Lake. Clever interactive games, videos, and mechanical displays complete the picture. This is a nice way to wrap up a day that has taken you past three of the system's projects.

I-5 will bring you back to the L.A. area or north to Bakersfield and beyond.

In the Area

Lake Castaic, 32132 Ridge Route Road, Castaic, CA 91384. 805-257-4050.

Rock Inn, 17539 Elizabeth Lake Road, Lake Hughes, CA 93532. 805-723-1855.

Pyramid Lake, Smokey Bear exit, I-5. Mail address: Box 249, Piru, CA 93040. 805-295-1245.

Vista del Lago Visitors Center, Vista del Lago exit, I-5. Mail address: Box 98, Castaic, CA 91384. 805-294-0219.

Fort Tejon State Historic Park, Fort Tejon exit, I-5. Mail address: Box 895, Lebec, CA 92343. 805-248- 6692.

Hungry Valley, Gorman, CA 93243. 805-248-7007.

13 ~ Road to Shangri-la

From Santa Paula to Ojai and Carpinteria

Getting Started: From Ventura, take State 126. Exit at Tenth Street in Santa Paula.

Route: From Santa Paula, follow State 150 to Ojai and Carpinteria. About thirty-five miles.

Highlights: *Stroll an old-fashioned American Main Street and visit the Union Oil Museum to learn how California's oil industry was born. Lose yourself in peaceful lemon groves. Watch the antique planes take off at Santa Paula Airport. Then drive over the mountain to the hidden Ojai Valley and down to sparkling Carpinteria Beach.*

Begin at Tenth and Main Streets, the power corner where the headquarters of Santa Paula's citrus and oil industries stood side by side for years, dictating the fortunes of the Santa Clara Valley. Today the Limoneira Company, whose 4,000 acres of fruit trees made Santa Paula the lemon capital of the world, has moved its offices out to the groves themselves. Union Oil Company has headquarters in another city. But the imposing two-story brick-and-sandstone Union Oil Building from 1888, with the American flag flying from its turret, was turned into the intriguing Union Oil Museum in 1990.

The papers of incorporation of the petroleum giant were signed upstairs in this building in 1890, years after California's first commercially successful oil well was drilled in nearby Sisar Canyon.

Make it a point to visit the museum, especially with school-age children in tow. The ground floor that once housed company offices is now a state-of-the-art popular science gallery with interactive displays. You can try your luck at striking it rich in a wildcatting video game or push a button that sends a miniature drill through deep rock strata while you watch. An exhibit of fossil shells shows how geologists use them to find rich oil deposits. A full-scale thirties gas station in the far corner brings a smile.

When you're done, follow Tenth Street one block north to Santa Barbara Street. Alongside the tracks where it was built in 1886 is the old Southern Pacific depot, now home to the Chamber of Commerce and the local art association. The spreading Moreton Bay fig tree across from the depot is even older. It was planted in 1879 on Independence Day. You might enjoy the long red barn housing the Mill, a garden supply and feed store one block up on Mill Street. It mixes merchandise for sale with memorabilia that looks as if the owners have never thrown anything out since the store opened for business in 1885.

While on Mill Street, you'll see the imposing half-timbered Glen Tavern Inn from 1911. It was built to accommodate visiting oil and citrus bigwigs who arrived at the depot in increasing numbers as Santa Paula's oil and citrus fortunes grew. Later, Hollywood discovered this piece of small-town America, and luminaries such as Harry Houdini, Rin TinTin, Clark Gable, and Carole Lombard are listed on the carefully preserved guest register. The tavern, a National Historic Landmark, is a bed and breakfast with recently remodeled rooms, but the Victorian lobby is still a step back in time.

If you're making this trip in October or from Thanksgiving through December 22, you're in for an old-fashioned country treat at the Faulkner Farm. The Addams family would feel right at home at this old-time farmstead, a three-story gingerbread extravaganza from 1894. Allan Ayers, a Faulkner descendant, grows pumpkins and Christmas trees in the fields. He opens the farm (though not the house) during pumpkin and Christmas tree seasons for hayrides, Model T rides, pumpkin-carving contests, caroling, two-stepping, and other holiday fun. If you want to take home pumpkins or a Christmas tree, you go out and harvest your own. To get there, take State 126 to Briggs Road north and go one-quarter mile to the farm.

The Faulkner Farm

Lovers of antique airplanes will enjoy the private Santa Paula Airport. Drive south from downtown on Eighth Street. You might be just in time to catch the antique air show, held the first Sunday of every month from 10:00 A.M. to 2:00 P.M. At other times, a good place to watch the old planes going through their paces is from Logsdon's Restaurant at the airport, which looks right out on the runways. In town, a favorite place to eat since the thirties has been Familia Diaz at Tenth and Harvard.

To drive out of Santa Paula, take Tenth Street, which becomes Ojai Road (State 150). Follow it north for thirteen miles past oak-covered hills, farmers' fields, Christmas tree farms, cutting horse ranches, and roadside fruit and vegetable stands. You're on your way to the magical valley that film director Frank Capra chose as his stand-in for Shangri-la in his classic *Lost Horizon* with Ronald Colman. The two-lane road climbs swiftly past the suburban groves and gardens into real ranch country. When the road swings west to skirt the flank of Sulphur Mountain (roll up your windows if you don't like the smell of rotten eggs), look for the blackish oil seeps on the sides of the hills. Long before geologists hiked into these hills, Chumash Indians were using this asphalt to waterproof their pitch baskets and for medicine and body paint.

The road flattens out through the farmland of the prosperous upper Ojai Valley. Then it loops around the side of Black Mountain before starting a stunning descent. Be sure to stop at the turnout marked "The Ojai Valley" before continuing down Dennison Grade. That's the vantage point where Ronald Colman first saw Shangri-la. Ordinary mortals can sit on the cement bench and enjoy a bird's-eye view of the graceful seven-mile-long valley, with its rows of orange and lemon trees. To the west, cradling the valley from Pacific winds, stands the Nordhoff Range, and to the east are the towering Topa Topas. The natural beauty of this mountain-fast valley has attracted a large artists' colony, the exclusive Thacher

School, Sheila Cluff's Oaks at Ojai spa, and two world-famous philosophy centers, the Krishnamurti Foundation and the Krotona Institute of Theosophy.

Once you've reached the valley floor and passed Boccali's restaurant (Ojai people just call it the pizza place), keep heading through the sun-kissed groves and horse ranches until you reach town. The pleasing harmony of downtown architecture along Ojai Avenue (State 150) is no accident. Ojai's colonnaded buildings were the pet project of early valley aficionado glass magnate Edward Drummond Libbey of the Libbey-Owens-Ford Company. In 1916, he built the town's distinctive mission-style shopping arcade and the old Spanish post office tower at Signal Street and Ojai Avenue (still the only traffic light in town). The Oaks at Ojai, kitty-corner to the post office, occupies Libbey's Oaks Hotel. The celebrated Ojai Music Festival, held in early June, takes place at the Libbey Bowl in Libbey Park across from the arcade.

You can learn more about Ojai's Chumash Indian past through a beautiful display of baskets and other artifacts at the Ojai Valley Museum in a former fire station on Montgomery Street. Ojai's present can be seen through the paintings and sculptures by local artists at the Art Association next door. There are galleries all over town and a big concentration of them at the arcade, which also will keep you busy going through the sophisticated merchandise in the shops. The shops continue on in the streets behind the arcade. When you're ready for light refreshment, try the unpretentious Plaza Pantry on Matilija Street. Walk through the arches and look for the Union Jack. The proprietor has been serving scones and tarts here for more than fifteen years. The Chamber of Commerce has an office at the start of the arcade, at 338 East Ojai Avenue. Stop in to pick up maps and hotel, restaurant, and shopping guides.

There are more than thirty-five restaurants in the Ojai Valley. For pizza, it's Boccali's. For weekend lunch on a flower-filled patio, try the contemporary European cooking at Suzanne's Cuisine on West Ojai Avenue or the Belgian cooking of L'Auberge on El Paseo. (Midweek, these restaurants serve dinner only.) If you plan to stay the night, two outstanding choices are the luxurious Ojai Valley Inn, with golf and tennis (another Libbey contribution), at the west end of town and the antique-filled old Theodore Woolsey House to the east, where you drove in.

Even on a day trip, you can get a feeling for the good life in this valley among the citrus groves and horse farms by getting out into the country, which is never far away in Ojai. Go back east on Ojai Avenue (State 150) to Boccali's and turn left on Reeves Road. Turn left again on McAndrew Road to the serene grounds of the Krishnamurti Foundation. Continue to the end of McAndrew to the 400-acre campus of the Thacher School. Take Thacher Road west and turn left on Carne Road for the return to Ojai Avenue.

Leave town on State 150 heading down the seventeen miles to Carpinteria, a gem of a south-facing beach in a small town wedged between Santa Barbara and Ventura. On the outskirts of Ojai, you'll see a stand of eucalyptus trees on your left. The Ojai Valley Inn is just behind them up Country Club Drive. Shortly after, you'll notice State 33 on your right. You can make a delightful detour by turning north toward the mountains on State 33 to the venerable Wheeler Hot Springs spa for hot and cold mineral baths in an unusual palm tree oasis. The restaurant there is housed in an 1891 lodge. It is open from Thursday through Sunday for dinner and for weekend brunch between 10:00 A.M. and 2:30 P.M.

Back on State 150 it's only a few miles down Casitas Pass to man-made Lake Casitas, whose shoreline zigzags among oak-covered hills. This was the site of the canoeing and rowing events for the 1984 Los Angeles Olympics. In recent years, anglers have pulled twenty-one-pound bass, forty-two-pound channel catfish, and nine-pound trout out of this lake, but unless you plan to fish or camp, pass up the turnoff and drive on down the hill. You'll get excellent views of the lake's complicated thirty-two-mile shoreline from below.

Between here and Carpinteria, the road cuts down through avocado groves, with their spreading trees planted in patterns that resemble giant vineyards. The trees climb to the crests of the hills, extending out of sight.

When you reach the ocean, with its offshore oil islands ranged like battleships on maneuvers, cross US 101 to the coastal road and turn right on the street with the "Services" sign. You'll soon be on Carpinteria Avenue, heading for "the world's safest beach," Carpinteria State Beach. Go left on the town's small main street, Linden Avenue, to where the road ends at a mile-long stretch of clean white sand bordering calm, shallow ocean waters. The Channel Islands off the coast, acting as a buffer, and a 2,000-foot reef sloping down from the shore keep the surf down. To reach the entrance to the Carpinteria State Beach camping and picnic grounds, where you may want to park, take Carpinteria Avenue to Palm Avenue.

If you want to stay over, try the Best Western Carpinteria Inn on Carpinteria Avenue. For enchiladas and karaoke, the hot spot is Chuy's down the street. To catch US 101 home, go back the way you came and follow the signs to the freeway.

In the Area

Santa Paula Chamber of Commerce, Tenth and Santa Barbara Streets, Santa Paula, CA 93060. 805-525-5561.

Santa Paula Union Oil Museum, 1001 Main Street, Santa Paula, CA 93060. 805-933-0076.

Santa Paula Airport, Eighth and Santa Maria Streets, Santa Paula, CA 93060. 805-933-1155.

Faulkner Farm, 14292 West Telegraph Road, Santa Paula, CA 93060. 805-525-9293.

Familia Diaz Restaurant, Tenth and Harvard Streets, Santa Paula, CA 93060. 805-525-2813.

Glen Tavern Inn, 134 North Mill Street, Santa Paula, CA 93060. 805-933-3777.

Logsdon's Restaurant, 834 East Santa Maria Street, Santa Paula, CA 93060. 805-525-1101.

Ojai Chamber of Commerce, 388 East Ojai Avenue, Ojai, CA 93023. 805-646-8126.

The Oaks at Ojai, 122 East Ojai Avenue, Ojai, CA 93023. 805-646-5573 or 800-752-6257.

Ojai Valley Museum, 109 South Montgomery Street, Ojai, CA 93023. 805-646-2290.

Boccali's Restaurant, 3277 Ojai Avenue, Ojai, CA 93023. 805-646-6616.

Ojai Valley Inn, Country Club Drive, Ojai, CA 93023. 805-646-5511 or 800-422-6524.

L'Auberge, 314 El Paseo, Ojai, CA 93023. 805-646-0288.

Plaza Pantry, 221 East Matilija Street, Ojai, CA 93023. 805-646-6325.

Suzanne's Cuisine, 502 West Ojai Avenue, Ojai, CA 93023. 805-640-1961.

Theodore Woolsey House, 1484 East Ojai Avenue, Ojai, CA 93023. 805-646-9779.

Wheeler Hot Springs, 16825 Maricopa Highway, Ojai, CA 93023. 805-646-8131 or 800-994-3353.

Carpinteria State Beach, 5361 Sixth Street, Carpinteria, CA 93013. 805-684-2811.

Chuy's, 5096 Carpinteria Avenue, Carpinteria, CA 93013. 805-682-2444.

Best Western Carpinteria Inn, 4558 Carpinteria Avenue, Carpinteria, CA 93013. 805-684-0473

14 ~

Of Stagecoaches and Vines

From San Marcos Pass to the Santa Ynez Valley

Getting Started: From US 101, take State 154 in Santa Barbara.

Route: From Santa Barbara, State 154 goes through the towns of Santa Ynez, Ballard, and Los Olivos. Continue on State 154 to Foxen Canyon Road. About fifty miles.

Highlights: *Climb 2,000 feet into the mountains behind Santa Barbara. Puzzle out the meaning of 400-year-old cave paintings. Retrace a stagecoach route and visit century-old taverns along the way. Relax in the country towns of the Santa Ynez Valley. End with a winery tour in scenic Foxen Canyon.*

State 154 shoots up through the San Marcos Pass in the Santa Ynez Mountains. As red-tiled roofs, orange groves, and ocean fall away below, watch for Painted Cave Road on the right. Now steel yourself for two miles of narrow going on a road that spirals sharply uphill without guardrails. Look for the modest sign to the Chumash Painted Cave. Although the cave is a State Historic Park, there's no parking lot and no park. Find a place on the narrow shoulder of the road and climb the short, rocky path to the mouth of the cave. It's a shallow cave, about fifteen feet high, but its entrance is closed off by an iron grille to protect the precious paintings from vandals, who have already ruined some of the wall. You can make out the primitive animal outlines and strange geometric forms in black, white, and ocher if you peer into the cave and wait for your eyes to get used to the dark. Archaeologists don't know for sure what message the Chumash meant to leave here 400 years ago. They think that the black-and-white circle might be an artist's depiction of a solar eclipse that was recorded here in the seventeenth century.

The road doesn't get any better when you leave the cave, but at least it's only another mile uphill before you turn left on Camino Cielo (Sky Road), where you can look down into the Santa Ynez Valley. Camino Cielo leads back to State 154. Turn right to go over the 2,225-foot summit and then left onto narrow Stagecoach Road. You'll get only a snippet of the road that coach passengers endured because just around the bend is a sight that has warmed travelers' hearts for more than a century. The weathered old log-and-stone Cold Spring Tavern, in a nest of sycamores and oaks, was a welcoming watering place for horses and humans on the route between Santa Maria and Santa Barbara. The narrow-gauge Pacific Coast Railway would take travelers as far south as the Santa Ynez Valley, dropping them off at Mattei's Tavern across from the Los Olivos depot. From there they would transfer to sturdy stages, called mud wagons. They stopped to fortify themselves at Cold Spring Tavern before the last pull up over the mountain and down to Santa Barbara.

The original tack room is now the bare, barnlike Wagon Wheel Back Bar, crowded with beer-drinking bikers on weekends. Next to it, known in the 1880s as the Cold Stream Relay Station, is a cozy, low-ceilinged log cabin restaurant. Its several small dining rooms have their own stone fireplaces. Hunting trophies hang on the walls, and the door handles are stag horns. Santa Barbara residents regularly run up here for lunch or for a candlelight dinner from an eclectic menu that includes venison, buffalo, quail, and rabbit. The atmosphere is so mesmerizing that you'll be startled by the sight of the telephone booth outside the door.

As you turn left out of the parking lot to follow Stagecoach Road back to State 154, you'll see a modern wonder—the green steel span of the Cold Spring Arch Bridge—looming over you. The bridge was built along State 154 to cut off some rough canyon stretches. At the bottom of the hill, you can

Bass fishermen on Lake Cachuma

detour to the right on Paradise Road, which leads into the golden hills of Paradise Valley.

Stop at the Los Prietos Ranger Station six miles along for information on Los Padres National Forest and its campgrounds on the shore of the Santa Ynez River. Much of Santa Barbara's unspoiled backcountry lies within this second largest national forest in California. It was named in the 1930s for the Franciscan mission fathers.

If you've taken this detour, double back and follow Paradise Road all the way to State 154, then turn right onto the highway. If you're still at the bottom of Stagecoach Road, turn left on Paradise Road and right on State 154. After several pleasant sets of rolling hills, you'll come over a rise to spot Lake Cachuma, named for the Chumash Indian village that was sacrificed for the lake. Fishermen claim that the lake's irregular bottom accounts for its oversize bass. There's no swimming (this is Santa Barbara's reservoir), but there are pool facilities and extensive county campgrounds. To view the lake and its long Bradbury Dam at their best, drive farther down the highway past the entrance to the long, narrow access road on your right.

From here it's only a short way to the idyllic green hills and fences of horse country. The town of Santa Ynez is one of five valley towns, each with its own history and personality. Santa Ynez is a ranching center with a false-front western downtown. Solvang celebrates its Danish roots in grand style. Los Olivos is a trove of old Victorian houses. Buellton, home of the first Andersen's split pea soup restaurant, is motel city. And tiny Ballard has the "little red schoolhouse."

When you see the sign to State 246, you're in Santa Ynez. Turn left on State 246, right on Edison Street, and right on Sagunto Street, the town's center. Shops in Santa Ynez advertise their wares: horsemen's supplies, building materials, and ostrich burgers. It's the kind of place where you'll find a hay truck parked in front of the Maverick Saloon during the noonday break. A number of ranches have begun breeding ostriches for their extra-lean meat. These doe-eyed creatures look at you from behind fences where horses once stood.

Santa Ynez's biggest tourist draw is the Parks-Janeway Carriage House, in a big, airy shed just up the block. Its collection of thirty-five wagons and carriages in mint condition makes it one of the top ten carriage museums in the nation. Transportation buffs will have a field day examining the Yosemite Stage and Turnpike Company coach, which transported tourists from the San Joaquin Valley to Yosemite in the early 1900s, or the 1895 British game-hunting cart with compartments under the seats for the hounds. The stagecoaches on display are awesome in size.

Next door, the Santa Ynez Valley Historical Museum has worthwhile exhibits that tell the history of the area through displays of Chumash baskets and pots, a collection of cattle brands, and model rooms showing a typical pioneer house. The museum is open Friday through Sunday from 1:00 to 4:00 P.M. The Carriage House also is open Tuesday through Thursday from 10:00 A.M. to 4:00 P.M.

Even if you're not in the mood for refreshments, you simply must walk one block farther on Sagunto Street to the Painted Ladys Tea Room in the pretty pink house with hunter green trim surrounded by a ragtag English garden. Women are invited to choose a feather boa and Victorian hat from a box of antique clothing at the door to wear while dining. The tearooom serves breakfast, lunch, and tea, accompanied by home-baked scones and fruit breads, Wednesday through Sunday from 10:00 A.M. to 4:00 P.M.

The Santa Ynez Winery, opened in 1976, is one of the oldest wineries in the valley, unless you count the wines the padres produced back in the mission days. It's right outside of town and worth a detour. Turn back to State 246 and turn right. Go left on El Refugio Road and follow it to the vineyards. You'll see the winery's long gray building with a

Wine ages in barrels in a cool cellar at the Santa Ynez Winery

welcoming porch and picnic tables on the right. Inside this former dairy barn, you can taste the winery's best-known sauvignon blancs, chardonnays, and more and take a self-guided tour of the vines, grape crusher, fermenting tanks, and barrels, with the aid of an annotated map and answers supplied by a willing staff.

The Santa Ynez wineries don't have restaurants, but they do have pleasing picnic areas. To enjoy a newly purchased bottle on the spot, bring your own picnic. You can get a free map of the Santa Ynez wine country at most wineries, hotels, and tourist attractions or from the Santa Barbara County Vintners' Association.

Next stop is Ballard's "little red schoolhouse," which has been open for classes continuously since 1883. Drive back on El Refugio Road past the town of Santa Ynez and turn left on Baseline Avenue. Turn right on Cottonwood Street, and you'll come to Ballard's pride, the red wooden schoolhouse with steeple and school bell. Set back on a lush lawn and shaded by a pair of giant walnut trees, the one-room school, only slightly enlarged and kept up like a jewel, currently houses kindergarten and grades 1 and 2 of the contemporary Ballard School next door.

Swing back to Baseline Avenue and turn right. The inviting gray-and-white building on the left is the elegant fifteen-room Ballard Inn, a new building with a white picket fence and country flavor. Across from it is the popular Ballard Store Restaurant, in a remodeled thirties grocery. It's known for refined California cuisine and a good list of California wines.

From here you're on your way to Los Olivos, where the old Victorian houses lean to pink and robin's-egg blue. Turn right on Alamo Pintado Road and left on Grand Avenue, and you'll be at the flagpole in the middle of the village that doubled for small-town U.S.A. in Andy Griffith's *Return to Mayberry*. Los Olivos has a thriving artists' colony, and it's fun to gallery-hop along its quaint streets. On weekends, the streets are filled with city browsers. The one place you won't want to miss here is Mattei's Tavern. Drive a few blocks farther on Grand Avenue and watch for the narrow frontage road called Railway Avenue on the left, the last street before the highway. The long, white two-story building, with the Stars and Stripes and the California bear flag flying, still says "California Stage Office" on the door. In the early days, it served passengers as restaurant, saloon, hotel, ticket office, and waiting room. Now it's a dinner house and convivial bar done in lace curtains, wicker, and velour. Portraits of the original nineteenth-century innkeepers hang above the fireplace in the parlor.

From here you're headed for the Foxen Canyon wine trail to sample some wine, view the winemaking process, or simply enjoy the classic California scenery of gentle hills and spreading oaks. On leaving the tavern, drive the few yards to rejoin State 154. Turn left and then right onto Foxen Canyon Road. The road rises into magnificent ranch land before diving down to meet a valley of vines. At Zaca Station Road, a wooden sign directs you to the wineries along the trail. Most of them are to the right, but the one that first put Santa Ynez on the wine map is perched on a hilltop one mile to the left.

The award-winning Firestone Vineyard, with 270 acres of grapes, is the largest holding in the area. It is owned by a scion of the Firestone Tire and Rubber family who came to the valley in the early seventies and commissioned a stylish darkwood building that would be right at home in the Napa Valley. Park on the edge of the vineyards and go through the heavy wooden door to the central picnic garden. You can enter the tasting room through a small door on the left. The bartender will be pouring the day's selections from Firestone's highly respected list, headed by its chardonnay, Johannisberg Riesling, and merlot. The guided tour of the cellars and vineyards is one of the best.

The Fess Parker Winery is a glamorous addition to the Foxen Canyon wine trail. Go back to Zaca Road and continue straight on past the wine trail sign, where Zaca becomes Foxen Canyon Road. Parker's winery, looking like a country club, opened in 1992. It is surrounded by a regal expanse of lawn shaded by oaks. Parker's son is the winemaker, and Dad, whom you'll remember as Davy Crockett and Daniel Boone, drops in at the lavishly furnished salesroom to chat about his chardonnays and Johannisberg Rieslings. He'll autograph your bottle and his old Hollywood publicity stills. Tours of the winery are by appointment only.

A beautiful three-mile ride through pastureland leads to the Zaca Mesa Winery. You'll recognize it by the old windmill at the entrance to its oak-shaded hollow. Inviting picnic tables are massed in a wildflower garden outside the high-ceilinged tasting room, which looks out across a sunny valley. Among its consistent award winners are chardonnays, Pinot noirs, and Syrahs. The winery offers liberal pourings of its new releases and a comprehensive tour of the premises.

From here, Foxen Canyon Road leads to more wineries and vast vegetable farmland all the way to Santa Maria. Follow it for as long as you like. For a speedy way back to the Santa Barbara area, which is well worth an overnight stay, return to Zaca Station Road and connect with US 101.

In the Area

Cold Spring Tavern, 5995 Stagecoach Road, Santa Barbara, CA 93105. 805-967-0066.

Four Seasons Biltmore, 1260 Channel Drive, Santa Barbara, CA 93108. 805-969-2261.

Villa Rosa, 15 Chapala Street, Santa Barbara, CA 93101. 805-966-0851.

Santa Barbara County Vintners' Association, 3669 Sagunto Street, Unit 103, Santa Ynez, CA 93460. 805-688-0881.

Santa Ynez Winery, 343 North Refugio Road, Santa Ynez, CA 93460. 805-688-8381.

Santa Ynez Valley Historical Museum and Parks–Janeway Carriage House, 3596 Sagunto Street, Santa Ynez, CA 93460. 805-688-7889.

The Painted Ladys Tea Room, 3631 Sagunto Street, Santa Ynez, CA 93460. 805-686-5440.

Ballard Inn, 2436 Baseline Avenue, Ballard, CA 93463. 805-688-7770 or 800-638-2466.

Ballard Store Restaurant, 2449 Baseline Avenue, Ballard, CA 93463. 805-688-5319.

Ballard Schoolhouse, Schoolhouse Road, Ballard, CA 93463.

Mattei's Tavern, State 154, Los Olivos, CA 93441. 805-688-4820.

Firestone Vineyard, 5017 Zaca Station Road, Los Olivos, CA 93441. 805-688-3940.

Fess Parker Winery, 6200 Foxen Canyon Road, Los Olivos, CA 93441. 805-688-1545.

Zaca Mesa Winery, 6905 Foxen Canyon Road, Los Olivos, CA 93441. 805-688-9339.

15 ~

Flower Power

From Gaviota Pass to Jalama Beach, Lompoc, and Solvang

Getting Started: Take US 101 to State 1 at Gaviota Pass west of Santa Barbara.

Route: From Gaviota Pass, follow State 1 to Jalama Road and Lompoc. Then take Santa Rosa Road back to Solvang. About seventy-five miles.

Highlights: *Explore the wind-swept coast at hidden Jalama Beach. Tour the rainbow-colored flower fields of Lompoc. Walk in the footsteps of the padres at magnificent Mission La Purísima. Sample* smorrebrod *in Old World Solvang. Go anytime, but at least once, go at the height of flower season.*

The drive begins near Gaviota, where US 101 turns away from the coast, cutting off the southwest heel of Santa Barbara County. Just after US 101 comes out of the tunnel at Gaviota Pass, take the turnoff for State 1. Follow it for fourteen miles through the lima bean fields to Jalama Road. This undemanding bean takes well to dry farming, and farmers have brightened every level piece of this arid land with lima beans, garbanzos, and pinquitos, the local specialty.

Modest Jalama Road, coming up on your left, is the only road that goes down to the isolated coastline between Gaviota and Lompoc. There is no road along the coast, just the

Southern Pacific Railroad tracks. Only train passengers see the entire fifty miles of untouched sand and forbidding palisades.

Jalama Road leads down to one of California's best-kept secrets—a small, wild section of beach and cliffs at the southern tip of sprawling Vandenberg Air Force Base. At first the road runs docilely through a broad lima bean valley, but before you know it, the beans disappear and the road is wriggling through the rough coastal hills along narrow ridges and bottomless chasms. When the terrain calms down and the canyon oaks bow out in favor of furry chaparral, you'll know that the ocean is just over the ridge.

Both windsurfers and board surfers find ideal conditions at Jalama Beach. When the surf is up, you'll come upon a row of cars parked at the top of the road, where the surfers suit up before climbing down to catch the waves off Tarantula Point.

Drive down past the railroad tracks and through the gate of Jalama Beach County Park. If you wonder how the herd of motor homes lined up in the campgrounds ever made it over that road, the answer is practice; once they've discovered Jalama, they come back every year.

The riptides are too treacherous for swimming, but you can go surf-fishing or comb the dunes for jade, shells, and flotsam. During February and March and from September through November, bring binoculars for the parade of migrating gray whales spouting just beyond the breaking waves.

At the north end of the grounds, a quiet estuary is a haven for protected birds. Watch for great blue herons, ospreys, snowy egrets, and brown pelicans among the reeds.

Beyond the estuary to the north, a succession of steep-walled canyons, waves crashing at their base, marches toward Point Arguello. Beyond that is Honda Point, site of the Honda tragedy, in which seven U.S. Navy destroyers were wrecked on the rocks one stormy night in 1923. You can read the chilling details in a faded copy of the *Lompoc Record* posted on the wall of the park's snack shop.

You'll be going there for your Jalamaburger, which has become a local food legend. Kids in Lompoc and Santa Barbara drive here just to get one. Perhaps it's the sea air or the cook's "secret" sauce that has made this juicy burger so popular. *Sunset* magazine has ranked the Jalamaburger among its "Best in the West."

On the way out, the now-familiar Jalama Road will be easier to navigate. At State 1, continue on for about five miles through the mountains to Lompoc. Those white streaks in the hills aren't patches of snow. The Lompoc hills have the world's largest deposit of diatomaceous earth, or silica, which, like Lompoc's famous flowers, is a mainstay of the local economy. The powdery white earth is formed by the remains of one-cell plants that lived here 12 million to 15 million years ago when this area was the floor of a shallow ocean. The silica has prodigious filtering powers and is used for swimming pool filters, drugs, toothpaste, and hundreds of other products, including the yellow paint used for the stripe down the middle of the road on which you're driving.

We hope you'll forgive Lompoc for putting one of its unsightly diatomaceous earth refineries right at the entrance to Ocean Avenue (State 246). We know you will when you see the rainbow of flowers behind it. From May through September, dazzling blues, purples, lilacs, pinks, yellows, golds, oranges, and reds lie in wide symmetrical bands across the open fields. On the last weekend in June, the whole town is dazzlingly decked out for the Lompoc Flower Festival, with flower-covered floats, marching bands, equestrian parades, a carnival, and bus tours of the fields. Even if you can't make it for thė festival, you can take your own nineteen-mile tour past miles of sweet peas, petunias, asters, marigolds, nasturtiums, lavender, poppies, calendulas, and larkspurs—up to thirty varieties in endless colors and perfumes.

Pick up a map of the flower fields at the Chamber of Commerce, at 111 South I Street, or at the Mission La Purísima gate. Each year the map is updated to allow for crop rotation. Except for the flowers that decorate the floats, you really don't see cut flowers here. Lompoc's two big wholesale growers, Denholm Seeds and Bodger Seeds, grow flowers strictly for seeds, which they market worldwide. The greenhouses along the road are bedding plant nurseries, hidden behind white plastic walls.

The town of Lompoc is one mile down Ocean Avenue to the left. The most extensively restored California mission, La Purísima Concepción, is a couple of miles to the right. You'll need at least two hours to enjoy the mission. Turn right on Ocean Avenue and follow it to Mission Gate Road. You'll see a big wooden cross on the hill that, a guide explains, served as an early motel sign, showing weary travelers the way to a good night's rest.

Of all the twenty-one Franciscan missions from San Diego to Sonoma, the eleventh, La Purísima, gives the best picture of the role of the mission in early California. It is set amid almost 1,000 acres of ranch land and chaparral-covered hills that suggest the kind of isolation that missions mercifully relieved in those days. La Purísima's thick adobe walls and hand-hewn rafter logs bound together by animal hide look just as they did in the prosperous 1820s. Yet in the little entrance museum, you will see photos of La Purísima in almost total decay. It was abandoned and left to crumble after an Indian uprising wrecked it and the secularization of California mission lands in the 1830s finished it off. So what you see today is actually a faithful replica, built by the Civilian Conservation Corps in the 1930s.

The present reincarnation no longer belongs to the Catholic Church but is a State Historic Park and living history museum recalling the days when 1,000 Chumash Indians toiled in the mission cornfields, vineyards, vegetable gardens, corrals, and workshops. Animals they would have had, such as the four-horned churro sheep, longhorn cattle, goats, burros, horses, and pigs, stand inside crude wooden pens. The gardens are planted with traditional herbs and fruits such

There were no benches at La Purísima Concepción. Men stood on one side and women on the other, sitting or kneeling on the floor during Mass

as rosemary and sage, figs and grapes. Narrow earthen trenches carry water across the fields. Hides, highly valued for trade during mission days, hang in the sun to dry. Notice the three church bells in the graceful tower beside the church. The two side by side are the bronze originals, but the top bell is a wooden stand-in, which missions would use when a metal bell was missing.

Your own tour of the mission's painted church and thirty-six fully furnished rooms (such as the barracks, candle-making shop, forge, and kitchen) is a look into the past. It's especially fun when the mission comes to life and docent Indians, soldiers, and padres go about their daily work. These Mission Life Days are usually held one Saturday a month from April through August. A schedule is available from the State Park office. The park maintains twelve hiking trails into the wilderness on mission grounds and a well-shaded picnic area near the entrance.

When you leave the mission to tour the flowers, be sure to stop in downtown Lompoc on your way to the sweet pea fields west of town. A novel public mural project has made the walls of the downtown buildings into a visual history of the area. A mural guide is available at the Chamber of Commerce, at 111 South I Street. It leads you past gigantic portrayals of early Lompoc, including Chumash life, the diatomaceous earth and flower industries, and the mission. Our favorite is the tongue-in-cheek masterpiece on the parking lot side of the Sleep Shop at 137 South H Street. Lompoc was founded as a temperance colony in 1874, and in this mural the good women of Lompoc are shown ridding the town of demon rum. One woman is taking an ax to an offending barrel.

During your tour, you'll be right near the Lompoc Museum, at 200 South H Street, one of the few remaining Carnegie-endowed museums in the country. The in-depth display of Chumash Indian artifacts and the exhibits on the seed industry and the peculiar diatomite live up to the promise of the small, stately building.

Often visitors come to Lompoc hoping to tour nearby Vandenberg Air Force Base. Tours are held only on Friday, and reservations must be made at least a week in advance.

When Lompoc people drive to Solvang, they make it in less than half an hour on State 246. The scenic route takes a little longer but goes through eighteen miles of flower and vegetable fields in the sheltered Santa Rosa Valley. From Ocean Avenue, turn right (south) on State 1 and watch for Santa Rosa Road on the left. In July, the fields are ablaze with asters and zinnias, and in August you'll have half the world's supply of hybrid marigolds blooming right outside your car window. Turn east on State 246, which becomes Mission Drive as you approach the half-timbered Danish village of Solvang. At the statue of the Little Mermaid, like the one in Copenhagen harbor, turn right down Alisal Road, and you're in "Little Denmark."

This spotless village, with its imitation thatched roofs, storks' nests, and retired windmills, looks like a Hollywood movie set. But Solvang actually has its roots in the mother country. The town traces its history back to 1911 and the establishment of a Danish school dedicated to preserving folk traditions. The school is gone, but the traditions persisted as Solvang grew into a farming town and, in the 1940s, a day-tripper's paradise. A good part of the population is still of Danish descent, and many children take Danish language and history classes, keeping Old World traditions alive. The fun-filled Danish Days Festival, held the third weekend in September, recalls the customs of the town founders, with a parade, folk dancing, and Danish delicacies cooked and eaten on the street.

The rest of the year, 350 shops and restaurants supply treats and entertainment. The shop windows are crammed with carved wooden toys, hand-knit sweaters, children's costumes, Scandinavian cookware, and fine European glassware, china, and silver. Bakery windows have tempting displays of tarts, cakes, and cookies. And everywhere you look, you'll see sidewalk cafés.

Restaurants serve delectable open-faced sandwiches called *smorrebrod* and lavish smorgasbords (Scandinavian buffets). You'll find Danish meatballs, pickled red cabbage, boiled potatoes, light golden aebleskiver (dessert pancakes), and Danish beer on almost every restaurant menu. For a gala meal, try the smorgasbord or the regular menu at the Danish Inn Restaurant on Mission Drive.

When you think you've done the town, there's more. One block east of Alisal Road is Mission Santa Inés, nineteenth in the mission chain. (No one seems quite sure why Inez became Inés.) The authentically restored church, peaceful gardens, and Indian graveyard stand right across the parking lot from the tourist hoopla. When it was founded in 1804, the mission had a large Indian village and enough surrounding land to graze 13,000 cattle. Another interesting place to visit is Bethania Lutheran Church, at 603 Atterdag Road north of Mission Drive. In keeping with a rural tradition, it has a model sailing ship suspended over the sanctuary.

Solvang's shops close between 5:00 and 6:00 P.M., so if you arrive late in the day, it should be with dinner in mind. The town turns magical at twilight, when the tiny white Tivoli lights outline windows, doors, and rooftops. If you want to stay overnight, you'll find a large selection of hotels here and in nearby Buellton, or you can book a room at Solvang's new Storybook Inn bed and breakfast, which is just as charming as it sounds.

To return to US 101, follow State 246 to Buellton.

In the Area

Jalama Beach County Park, Star Route, Lompoc , CA 93436. 805-736-6316 or 805-736-3504.

Lompoc Valley Chamber of Commerce, 111 South I Street, Lompoc, CA 93438. 805-736-4567.

La Purísima Mission State Historic Park, 2295 Purísima Road, Lompoc, CA 93438. 805-733-3713.

Lompoc Museum, 200 South H Street, Lompoc, CA 93436. 805-736-3888.

Vandenberg Air Force Base, Western Spaceport Museum and Science Center, 2999 Lompoc-Casmalia Road, Lompoc, CA 93436. 805-736-6381.

Solvang Conference Center and Visitor Bureau, 1511 Mission Drive, Solvang, CA 93463. 800-946-3645.

Storybook Inn, 409 First Street, Solvang, CA 93463. 805-688-1703 or 800-786-7925.

Danish Inn Restaurant, 1547 Mission Drive, Solvang, CA 93463. 805-688-4813.

Mission Santa Inés, 1760 Mission Drive, Lompoc, CA 93463. 805-688-4815.

Index

Country Towns of Pennsylvania
Country Towns of Southern California
Country Towns of Texas
Country Towns of Vermont

In the 52 Weekends series:
52 Florida Weekends $12.95
52 Illinois Weekends
52 Indiana Weekends $12.95
52 Michigan Weekends
52 New Jersey Weekends $12.95
52 New York Weekends
52 Northern California Weekends $12.95
52 Virginia Weekends $12.95
52 Wisconsin Weekends

In the Natural Wonders series:
Green Guide to Hawaii
Natural Wonders of Alaska
Natural Wonders of Connecticut & Rhode Island
Natural Wonders of Florida
Natural Wonders of Georgia $12.95
Natural Wonders of Idaho
Natural Wonders of Maine
Natural Wonders of Massachusetts
Natural Wonders of Michigan
Natural Wonders of New Mexico $12.95
Natural Wonders of New Hampshire
Natural Wonders of New Jersey
Natural Wonders of New York
Natural Wonders of Northern California $12.95
Natural Wonders of Ohio
Natural Wonders of Oregon $12.95
Natural Wonders of Southern California
Natural Wonders of Texas
Natural Wonders of Vermont $12.95
Natural Wonders of Virginia
Natural Wonders of Washington $12.95
Natural Wonders of Wisconsin

Along the Shore:
California Under Sail
Florida Under Sail
New England Under Sail $12.95
Maine: Cruising the Coast by Car
New York–New Jersey Coastal Adventures

2

She learns to eat off the land.
He is a dinner plate in denim jeans.
She's 17 and starving
and clumsy with her mouth.
He is topless and rides bareback.
He has long hair and a bone necklace.
He whips up horses for her amusement.
They stampede around her like a lasso.
Her chest tightens. She feels like
an indigenous goddess
sitting on an upturned yellow bucket.
She laughs and he is inspired by the way
she sticks her tongue out. He comes
from a line of master carvers. Commits
their names into a kōwhai tree.
Reads a Hone Tuwhare poem. Gets her
underwear off. Teaches her how to canter
as an excuse to masturbate her. Is scared
of her parents—her white veteran father
with his fruity foreign accent and her mother
who wears Chanel and paints her eyebrows on
like an angry seagull ready to pick
at a carcass. Her mother, who makes them
pick fresh watercress to take back to the city
and watches them weave through the stream
in Levis cut at the thighs while she hovers
on the shore just like the metallic dragonflies,
bothersome all summer.

3

Her parents are thankful for the repaired
economy. Increased security. An inner-city
dwelling. And a yellow sports car to visit
the East Coast in the summer.
They love their lovely daughter.
They call her pretty but a worry.
They say she doesn't care about stability
or the sacrifices that they've made.
She just wants to make love again
in the stables. Suck Mick Jagger off
at Woodstock. Wear a black velvet mini
and a beret. Kiss her East Coast cowboy
like a groupie. He chops wood and makes
guitars. Plays the piano and the sax. Has a band
with his cousins. Won't make it very far.
Can play any kind of instrument with
hands like that. Overheard a girl at the town hall
call him the *Māori God of Music.*
Always another girl. Always another summer.
Explained to her by her mother, who had looked
relieved when the flush on her daughter's skin
finally wintered. Although it was glacier slow.
But every now and then something
still burns like a phantom limb.
So she gets rid of her Stevie Nicks dress.
Replaces it with a white one. Then a white one.
Until she has a closet full of expensive exoskeletons
satin   lace   pearl

that never quite fit right
and make an enemy
out of her body.

Receipt

It's just unsexy, you know, like when you tried to put me in the original tub with my wrists tied to either side of the broom. I didn't feel like Jesus Christ, or like Bettie Page, despite my haircut. More like a rotisserie chicken. Do you understand how hard it is to be a sex kitten when you have had your skin rubbed raw like poultry? Actually I felt more like a rubber duck. Sure the photos came out all right. I can edit out the red-slapped embarrassment, but you're no Irving Klaw. You're a family man with a volcanic complex. A little too interested in your interests if you know what I mean. More importantly who told you it was a good idea to get anybody a custom-made bathtub? It's weird. I would like to think it was romantic. But I'm already drowning in attention, I mean affection, and would prefer not to have access to the perfect facilities to finally do it in. It's a little too ironic if you know what I mean. Too permanent. I can't re-gift it. I can't even move it! It's bolted to your floor! And where would I put it? I don't have a garden at my tiny flat. I couldn't use it for compost, or growing melons or something. So really it was a gift for yourself. Maybe you'd have better luck trying to sell it off in Auckland. You're moving back there anyway. Overall, it's just the symbolism of it, you know, like what it represents. It sits there, expectant, a little bit like you, hoping I would spend my time in there holding my breath.

Identity Politics

I buy a Mana Party T-shirt from AliExpress.
$9.99 free shipping via standard post.
Estimated arrival 14–31 working days.
Tracking unavailable via DSL. Asian size XXL.
I wear it as a dress with thigh-high vinyl boots
and fishnets. I post a picture to Instagram.
Am I navigating correctly? Tell me,
which stars were my ancestors looking at?
And which ones burnt the black of searching irises
and reflected something genuine back? I look to
Rihanna and Kim Kardashian shimmering in
Swarovski crystals. Make my eyes glow with seeing.
I am inhaling long white clouds and I see
rivers of milk running towards orange oceans of
sunlit honey. Tell me, am I navigating correctly?
I want to spend my money on something bourgie,
like custom-made pounamu hoop earrings. I want to
make them myself but my line doesn't trace back
to the beauties in the south making amulets
with elegant fingers. I go back into blackness,
I go back and fill in the gaps, searching through archives
of advertisements: Welcome to the Wonderland
of the South Pacific. Tiki bars, traffic-light cocktails &
paper umbrellas. Tell me, am I navigating correctly?
Steering through the storm drunk & wet-faced
waking up to the taste of hangover, a dry mouth, a strange bed,
shirt above my head is the flag fluttering over everything.
What were we celebrating? The 6th of February is the anniversary
of the greatest failed marriage this nation has ever seen.

In America, couples have divorce parties. We always arrive fashionably late. Tell me, am I navigating correctly? The sea our ancestors traversed stretches out farther than the stars.

Hawaiki

My mother, tired
from pregnancy and being
alive, named her last son
Hawaiki
like the paradise.

Some people say
it is where we go
when we die.

They say we dive
straight off the edge
of Cape Reinga and into
the point where the sky
hangs so heavy with spirits
that it touches the sea.

Other people say
that is where we were
before we came here
by waka, or whale, or perhaps

that was where we were
before there was anything at all

where we meant something
before we discovered

like Eve
God's forbidden fruit
in the shape of an I.

I think
it must be a womb
where everything is born
and returns to.

Life and death
are the colour red.

They are the colour
of a cosmic heartbeat
rising on his fresh baby flesh

pinched between fingers
and kissed.

ACKNOWLEDGMENTS

Ngā mihi to my MA class, to my convenor Chris Price and my supervisor Louise Wallace, whose advice and feedback shaped this collection as I was writing it during my MA at the International Institute of Modern Letters. Tēnā rawa atu koe to the e hoa Raife, wtho was there every day, distracting me, during the writing of this book. Thank you to Te Herenga Waka University Press, especially to Fergus, Ashleigh and Kristen for taking me on in multiple senses lol. Thank you to John Freeman—the tautoko you have given my mahi has been nek level and I am deeply appreciative—and also, thanks to Simone Noronha and the team at Knopf, for this glamorous American edition. Thank you to my brothers and sisters, Aniqueja, Jordan, Izzy, Hawaiki and Ba. Finally, I mihi to my whakapapa of wahine toa. This pukapuka is dedicated to my mother, nana, nanny and great-grandmother Adrienne, Ingrid, Tina and Harata "Charlotte" Karaka Wanders (1926–2016). Ka nui taku aroha ki a koe. My love for you is endless.

NOTES

"Poūkahangatus" is a hybridised word of my own invention, phonetically mimicking "Pocahontas." It has no literal Māori translation, though "pou" in te reo Māori means pillar or pole, and "kaha" means power or strength.

"Red American Mustang" was written in response to the exhibition Wahine: Beyond the Dusky Maiden / Ki tua o te puhi kiri rauwhero held at the National Library, Wellington (June–August 2017). Specifically, it was prompted by a talk delivered by Dr. Arini Loader titled "Owning Our Dusky Selves: Sex, Skin, and Women's Business." The phrase "ocean . . . waiting to be entered" was lifted from her presentation.

A NOTE ABOUT THE AUTHOR

Tayi Tibble (Te Whānau ā Apanui/Ngāti Porou) is an indigenous writer and poet based in Te Whanganui a Tara, Aoteraroa. In 2017 she completed a master's degree in creative writing from the International Institute of Modern Letters, where she was the recipient of the Adam Foundation Prize. *Poūkahangatus* won the Jessie Mackay Best First Book of Poetry Award and the Ockham New Zealand Book Awards. Her most recent collection, *Rangikura,* was published in 2021. She works in publicity at Te Herenga Waka University Press.

A NOTE ON THE TYPE

This book was set in Scala, a typeface designed by the Dutch designer Martin Majoor (b. 1960) in 1988 and released by the FontFont foundry in 1990. While designed as a fully modern family of fonts containing both a serif and a sans serif alphabet, Scala retains many refinements normally associated with traditional fonts.

Composed by North Market Street Graphics,
Lancaster, Pennsylvania

Printed and bound by Friesens Altona, Manitoba

Designed by Betty Lew